· A HISTORY LOVER'S ·
GUIDE TO

MEMPHIS
& SHELBY COUNTY

· A HISTORY LOVER'S ·
GUIDE TO
MEMPHIS
& SHELBY COUNTY

BILL PATTON

THE
History
PRESS

Published by The History Press
Charleston, SC
www.historypress.com

First published 2020

Manufactured in the United States

ISBN 9781467142373

Library of Congress Control Number: 2019954263

Notice: The information in this book is true and complete to the best of our knowledge. It is offered without guarantee on the part of the author or The History Press. The author and The History Press disclaim all liability in connection with the use of this book.

CONTENTS

ACKNOWLEDGEMENTS

I'd like to thank the helpful staff of the Memphis and Shelby County Room at the Memphis Public Library and Information Center, especially G. Wayne Dowdy, an underappreciated Memphis treasure and inexhaustible font of knowledge. I'd also like to thank Shekinah Toebbe, who helped track down many of this book's historical photos.

Fourteen years ago, I was fortunate enough to be able to turn from one passion, the practice of law, to another, Memphis history, and start a tour company, Backbeat Tours. At Backbeat I'm grateful to have a staff of talented people, especially the irreplaceable Megan May, who bring these Memphis stories to life and inspire me every day. Finally, I'd like to thank my wife, Deborah: without her love and support, this book would not be possible.

INTRODUCTION

On a drizzly day in early April 1819, two men rode on the top of a flatboat down the Mississippi River and watched the thick, lush vegetation of the banks roll by. The land was densely wooded and otherwise featureless, until a line of bluffs appeared on the eastern bank. The boat's pilot, an experienced riverman who had made this trip numerous times before, steered close to shore, caught the eddy at the foot of the bluff and drifted into a wide marshy stream that entered the larger river. Planks were laid over the mud to higher, firmer ground, and the passengers clambered ashore. They walked to the top of a rise and took stock of their surroundings: a few houses, crudely built on the edge of the bluff overlooking the river, and in the distance, the remains of a blockhouse. And there were trees, lots of trees.

The men were actually looking for trees, or rather for one particular tree: a large white oak with the initials "JR" carved into the trunk. The tree marked the corner of a five-thousand-acre tract once owned by a North Carolina speculator named John Rice. The men—William Lawrence and Marcus Winchester, agents for the tract's current owners—were here to survey the property and stake out streets and lots of a new town.

Rice had been killed by Indians nearly thirty years earlier, and his heirs sold the claim for $500 to a young Nashville attorney, John Overton. Overton shared the tract with his good friend, Andrew Jackson, and three years later, Jackson in turn shared his interest with another friend,

Sketch by Charles Alexandre Leseur of the Memphis waterfront in April 1828. *Courtesy of Memphis and Shelby County Room, Memphis Public Library and Information Center.*

Revolutionary War veteran General James Winchester. With the price of cotton rising and land on the frontier being rapidly developed, they believed there was money to be made by planting a city on the Mississippi bluffs. Overton, Jackson and Winchester were optimistic about the success of their venture and were sure that their city would be one of the most important on the Mississippi. Looking upon the mighty river as the American Nile, they continued the Egyptian motif and named the city Memphis, after the Egyptian Old Kingdom city of pharaohs at the mouth of the Nile delta.

There was just one problem: they didn't actually own the land at all. Legally, it still belonged to the Chickasaw Nation.

Not ones to let a technicality stand in the way of making money, the trio of proprietors, through friends in the Tennessee legislature, lobbied Congress "to procure a relinquishment of the Chickasaw claim." Congress quickly appointed a commission to negotiate with the Chickasaw. The commissioners, to no one's surprise, were former Kentucky governor Isaac Shelby and Andrew Jackson. That Jackson stood to gain an enormous personal profit from any resulting treaty seemed not to be a matter of concern to anyone.

On the way to the treaty ground, Jackson and Shelby had agreed to go no higher than $300,000; Shelby even thought half that would do.

The Chickasaws, for their part, proved to be no pushovers—they had previous experience negotiating with the U.S. government, and with Andrew Jackson in particular—and after nearly two weeks the bidding reached as high as $280,000, payable in fourteen annual installments of $20,000. On the verge of an agreement, the Chickasaws asked for "one more cent." America was so strong and rich, they argued, what was one more cent? Jackson asked if that would do it, and the Chickasaws said yes. The commissioners agreed, and everyone shook hands all around, only to find out a bit later from the interpreters that what the Chickasaws meant by "one more cent" was an additional $20,000 installment payment. Jackson, desperate for a treaty, readily agreed, but Shelby was furious and flatly refused. The two argued bitterly and almost came to blows. Jackson threatened to sign the treaty himself and send it to Washington for ratification and then added that, if the fifteenth annual payment of $20,000 was the issue, he would sign a bond and promise to pay it personally. Though he still had misgivings, Shelby relented, and the Chickasaw Cession was signed on October 19, 1818.

On the bluffs the following spring, the two surveyors, Lawrence and General Winchester's son, Marcus, hurried to finish their task. Ratification of the treaty had sparked a land rush, and other surveyors were staking claims in the area, too. As Overton wrote, "If the country settles as fast as I think it will…we must not let the owners of property on the Bluffs of the Mississippi above us be beforehand in laying off towns, as it might damp the sale of ours."

Overton's town plan was fairly enlightened for its day, with broad streets, four public squares and a spacious promenade along the top of the bluff down the entire length of the riverfront. Still, it faced substantial opposition from squatters and Indian agents who had been living here, some of them for over twenty years, since the time of the Spanish. To ease tensions and start their venture on a positive note, the proprietors decided to donate lots to the existing residents.

On May 22, 1819, Lawrence and Marcus Winchester called everyone together to formally announce the proprietors' plans, convey lots in the new town and issue temporary certificates of title. The first lot, no. 53, at the southeast corner of Winchester and Front Streets, was given to Benjamin Foy, a magistrate under the Spanish who, though he had moved across the river, was still influential and greatly respected on the bluffs. The second lot, on Front Street at the south side of the alley between Concord and Overton Streets, was given to the widow Peggy Grace, who had come some years before with her husband and settled just north of the Gayoso Bayou; her lot would in a few years be the site of one of the city's first taverns. Thomas Carr, who had been passing through the previous fall with his brother Anderson when he heard news of the treaty and decided to stay, was granted two swampy acres on Main Street on condition that he drain the land, build a mill and a blacksmith's shop in one year and a cotton gin in two years. Various other conveyances were made, and Marcus Winchester served out plenty of whiskey shipped in by flatboat for the occasion.

A few months later, Overton prepared a petition for the residents to sign, and on November 24, 1819, the Tennessee legislature created Shelby County, the first county in the state wholly west of the Tennessee River.

And so it began.

Several of the new arrivals, including the Bettis family from South Carolina, brought with them cotton seed; the Carr brothers, from Virginia, had brought with them over forty slaves, importing the country's original sin into the founding of the city, something that would have profound effects down through the years.

Memphis, from the very beginning, was all about grit and grind. As late as 1835, bears still occasionally wandered into town, and the Gayoso Bayou south of Adams Avenue—today's Danny Thomas Boulevard— was "a dense thicket for all manner of varmint," in the words of one early resident. There were few roads and no bridges; the first houses were cabins with mud chimneys. "As to society," according to another resident, "there was none; nothing that deserved that name." Whiskey was cheap—twenty-five cents a gallon—and brawling was common; for entertainment, boys would beg their parents to let them go into town on Saturdays to see the fights. Nonetheless, the city, with its convenient eddy at the foot of the bluffs, became a favorite stop for flatboats and, later, the steamboat trade as well. By the end of the decade, it seemed that Overton's venture might succeed, that Memphis would flourish and become a city of consequence.

Almost all of the currents of Memphis history were present from the start, flavored, like barbecue, with the smoke of darker things: cotton and slavery and a struggle for justice and, threaded through all of it, a spirit of innovation, generosity and rebellion. On its bicentennial, Memphis is very much the same as it ever was; currently the twenty-sixth-largest urban area in America, it is nonetheless one of a handful of cities with a definite, unique vibe that sets it apart from any place else. According to the

Smithsonian, more songs have been written about Memphis or mention Memphis in the lyrics than any other city in the world. Because when you want to evoke an indefinable sense of both romance and grit, beauty and pain, of a place where the past haunts the present, sometimes just the word "Memphis" will do.

Memphis has come a long way in two hundred years and has a lot of stories to tell. The chapters that follow tell only a few of them.

1

THE RIVER

Without the river, there wouldn't be Memphis.

The Mississippi River is the fourth-longest river in the world behind the Amazon, the Nile and the Yangtze, beginning in Lake Itasca, Minnesota, and draining over 1.2 million square miles, or 41 percent of the North American continent—all or part of thirty-one states and two provinces of Canada. If you threw a stick into Lake Itasca, it would take nearly ninety days to reach the Gulf of Mexico.

In awe, perhaps, of its sheer size and power, the early European explorers reached for religious imagery to name the river: Hernando de Soto called it *El Rio del Espiritu Santo*, while the French explorer Jacques Marquette called it *La Rivière de l'Immaculée Conception*. Native Americans who lived on its banks took a more prosaic yet colorful approach and called it such names as Big Greasy River and Miserable Wretched Dirty Water River. What stuck, however, was the Ojibwa name *Misi-ziipi*, meaning simply Great River. By any name, the river was the lifeblood of Memphis in its earliest days, bringing wealth and commerce in the form of cotton to its wharves on flatboats and, later, on graceful steamboats. It has also brought war, disease and refugees in times of crisis. Though railroads and, more recently, the airport, have taken pride of place in the city's transportation industry, the river remains a vital thread running through the history of Memphis.

COBBLESTONES

Riverside Drive between Court Avenue and Beale Street

The Memphis riverfront bears little resemblance to the riverfront of 1819, 1860 or even 1900. Early accounts tell of a large stretch of flat ground called the batture, on which the Chickasaw planted maize and even had a racecourse for their horses. Later, the batture was all but gone, washed downstream, and the river came right to the base of the bluffs (which were much steeper than today); it returned sometime later and formed the steamboat landing.

The Memphis Landing—the city's nineteenth-century cobblestone river landing where cotton, goods and passengers were loaded and unloaded from boats—is the only one of its kind surviving in North America, and perhaps the world. Unlike landings in other major river cities such as Pittsburgh, Cincinnati, St. Louis or New Orleans, it has changed little over the years.

Stretching over six hundred yards along the river, it's made up of over 900,000 stones laid in a variety of different patterns. Over one hundred iron ring bolts and other nineteenth-century mooring fixtures remain embedded in the stones, a testament to the heavy use of the landing by steamboats and all kinds of river vessels.

Memphis river landing and cotton bales. *Courtesy of Memphis and Shelby County Room, Memphis Public Library and Information Center.*

The Memphis Landing of today is the surviving portion of two once distinct areas, the Beale Street or South Memphis landing, developed at the foot of Beale Street beginning in 1838, and, to the north, the Great Memphis Landing, first developed in the 1840s between Union and Jefferson Avenues and eventually stretching north to where the Pyramid stands today.

Before 1858, the two landings were simply narrow strips of silt and clay at the foot of the bluffs. Depending on the water level—which can vary considerably—river passengers and laborers were often forced to cross two to three hundred feet of mud before reaching solid ground. (A recent archaeological dig under the cobblestones found a great many shoes buried in the muck.) The rapid growth of steamboat traffic and the cotton trade in the 1850s made stabilization of the landings a priority; in 1858, the city voted to pave the Great Landing, and later Beale Street Landing, with cobblestones. Work began in 1859; interrupted by the outbreak of the Civil War, it was completed in 1881. Despite numerous repairs and alterations, large sections of the original cobblestone paving projects remain in place today.

The growth of the nation's railroads slowly diminished the importance of the landing, especially after the completion of the Frisco Railroad Bridge in 1892. Still, the river remained a necessary connection between the rich cotton plantations of the Mississippi and Arkansas delta and the industrialized North well into the twentieth century, and passenger steamers continued to use the landing until the 1930s.

MUD ISLAND

57 North Island Drive

Mud Island is not really an island at all but a peninsula of sand, gravel and silt where the Wolf River meets the Mississippi River. It first appeared briefly in the early 1900s but became permanent in the spring of 1912. Two years earlier, the U.S. Navy had towed a warship—the USS *Amphitrite*—up the Mississippi, hoping to install it in St. Louis as a reservist training ship. They got it as far as Memphis, where low water temporarily prevented any further progress. The ship was anchored about eighty yards off the bluffs with the intention of resuming its journey upstream when water levels were higher, but the plan was apparently abandoned, and there the *Amphitrite* sat, nearly forgotten, until March or April 1912, when it was towed back to New Orleans. In the meantime, a sandbar had formed underwater around it. When the ship was removed, the underwater bar remained, and the Mississippi floodwaters of April and May deposited so much more sand and silt on top of it that a long muddy spit of land was revealed when the waters receded. The river continued to add to its work, and by the following year, 1913, the new peninsula extended all the way past Beale Street. By the 1920s, it became apparent that it was a permanent fixture, and there it sat, muddy and ugly and covered by floodwater every spring. It became the home of hardy folk who took advantage of free land and lived (unlawfully) in shacks on stilts. From 1959 to 1970, a downtown airport with one runway operated on the island, with pontoon ferryboat service to the cobblestone landing.

It was seventy years before someone figured out what to do with it. With the building of the Hernando de Soto Bridge in the 1970s, the U.S. Army Corps of Engineers dredged a deep channel in the river and deposited the mud and silt on the island, finally raising the height enough to prevent it from annual flooding. Mud Island River Park was built soon afterward, followed by the upscale Harbor Town development. The park features nice views of the downtown skyline along with a fifty-foot "MEMPHIS" sign, a five-thousand-seat amphitheater and a Mississippi River museum that's definitely worth a look. The centerpiece of the park, though, remains the River Walk—a five-block-long reproduction of the lower Mississippi, tracing the course of the river from Cairo, Illinois, to the Gulf of Mexico with every sandbar, oxbow and topographic contour faithfully reproduced, complete with flowing water that rises and falls with the water level in the actual river. The park is open every day, though the museum is open only Thursday through Sunday.

FRISCO BRIDGE AND HARAHAN BRIDGE

235 Virginia Avenue West

Three bridges span the Mississippi near Chickasaw Heritage Park. The middle bridge and the oldest of the trio is the Frisco Bridge, known originally as the Great Bridge at Memphis. When it opened on May 12, 1892, it was the first bridge to cross the lower Mississippi River and the only bridge south of St. Louis at that time. Its construction was a monumental engineering achievement, 770 feet long and over 75 feet above the river, the highest of any bridge in the country at that time.

Frisco Bridge under construction, 1891. *Courtesy of Memphis and Shelby County Room, Memphis Public Library and Information Center.*

The bridge had a huge impact on the local economy and helped make Memphis one of the nation's fastest growing cities at the turn of the twentieth century. Prior to the construction of the bridge, small sections of train were ferried across the river on a sidewheeler steamboat, a time-consuming process to say the least. This new bridge established Memphis as one of the nation's premier transportation centers, a reputation the city continues to enjoy to this day.

The opening day of the bridge was a festive occasion, with fifty thousand people in attendance listening to speeches from mayors, governors and senators while they waited to see if the bridge could sustain the weight of the first train; many believed it would plunge into the river. Eighteen locomotives—manned entirely by volunteers—were joined together to make the first crossing. The train of engines proceeded slowly across, stopping at the center of each span to determine if the bridge pilings remained solid. Once safely to the Arkansas side, the engines roared back across the bridge at sixty-five miles per hour, to the delight of the crowd.

In 1913, construction began on the Harahan Bridge immediately to the north from the Frisco Bridge. It opened with two tracks of rail traffic in

July 1916 and added two lanes of automobile traffic in early 1917. The bridge carried motor vehicles on wooden roadways cantilevered like wings off each side of the railroad bridge until 1949. Crossing the bridge by car on wooden planks more than seventy feet above the river, protected only by a low wooden guardrail, was a white-knuckled experience for many drivers, especially those unlucky enough to be on the span when a freight train rumbled alongside. In 1928, sparks from a passing locomotive ignited the roadway planks, causing one of the city's most spectacular fires.

In 2016, the north side roadway was converted to a bike and pedestrian path called Big River Crossing. The bridge has great views of the river and the Memphis skyline and connects with a network of parks and bike and pedestrian trails on both sides of the river, well worth a visit.

TOM LEE PARK

Riverside Drive at Beale Street

Stretching nearly one mile along the riverbank south of Beale Street is Tom Lee Park, named for an African American man who saved the lives of thirty-two white passengers aboard the steamer *M.E. Norman* when it capsized on May 8, 1925. Lee, a levee worker, was on the river in a small open motorboat and witnessed the sinking of the steamer. Though he could not swim and risked capsizing his own boat, he pulled as many people as he could from the waters, ferried them to safety on a sandy riverbank and then set out

Tom Lee Park.
Author photo.

20

again and again until he rescued all he could find. As night fell, he gathered driftwood and made a fire for the survivors huddled on the beach and then set out in search of bodies.

When asked about his actions that day, Lee said simply, "I seen something that had to be done and I did it." He was honored as a hero by the city and was given a house in North Memphis, along with a trip to Washington, D.C., to meet President Coolidge. In the 1950s, the city erected a monument that praised him as "A Very Worthy Negro." In 2006, a new monument was dedicated to Lee, a larger-than-life image of him saving one of the victims. The statue is surrounded by thirty-two lights, representing each of the survivors he rescued.

HOPEFIELD, ARKANSAS

1700 Robinson Road, Marion, Arkansas

Immediately across the river from Memphis, the piers of the Hernando de Soto (Interstate 40) Bridge rest atop the former site of Hopefield, Arkansas, a small town that had grown up around a Spanish fort built after the Spaniards had ceded the east bank to the Americans. Benjamin Foy, the town's leading citizen, built a large red mansion atop an earthen mound that was a landmark for years until it was carried away in a flood. During the Civil War, the whole town of Hopefield was such a hotbed of Confederate guerrilla activity that the Union army finally crossed the river and burned it to the ground. Despite some attempts after the war to revive the town, a series of floods wiped out the new buildings and the site was abandoned.

Until the late 1800s, the fields in the vicinity of Hopefield were notorious as Memphis's dueling grounds. In 1801, Tennessee became the first state to outlaw dueling, but duels continued to be popular methods for settling disputes of honor in America, especially in the South, until well after the Civil War. Duels were fairly frequent in Memphis, and a short trip across the river to Arkansas or to a grove of oaks on the Hernando Road just across the Mississippi state line provided the convenient fiction that there was no violation of Tennessee law. George Phelan, a prominent attorney—his house, the historic Hunt-Phelan mansion on the east end of Beale Street, still stands—was a participant in one of the last recorded duels, in 1870.

CENTENNIAL ISLAND AND ISLAND 37

1 Corona Road, Corona, Tennessee

It's natural to think of the river as the boundary between Tennessee and Arkansas, but there are thousands of acres of land on the west—"Arkansas"—side of the river that are actually in Tennessee. The Mississippi River is a dynamic, unpredictable waterway, often cutting new channels and making—or destroying—islands and sandbars. Less than twenty miles north of the Hernando de Soto Bridge, opposite Meeman-Shelby Forest State Park in the far northwest corner of Shelby County, is a stretch of the river known as the Centennial Cutoff, named for when the river dramatically straightened itself during a storm in the centennial year of 1876.

Prior to that year, the river turned first west from its general southerly path, then north, then west again around Island 37, then south and east and north and northeast before resuming a southerly course, making a notorious and odd-shaped promontory jutting out from the Tennessee mainland known as the "Devil's Elbow." The distance around was more than twenty

Centennial Island. *Author photo.*

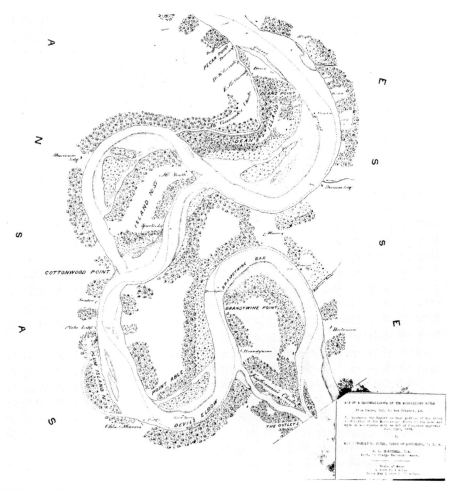

U.S. Army Corps of Engineers 1874 reconnaissance map of the Mississippi River, showing Island 37 and the Devil's Elbow. *Courtesy of Memphis and Shelby County Room, Memphis Public Library and Information Center.*

miles, though at its base the promontory was less than two miles wide. On the night of March 7, 1876, the river simply cut straight across the neck of the promontory and removed the tortuous bend.

One of the largest property owners in the Devil's Elbow, Memphis businessman John Trigg, lost over one thousand acres of land in a flash, while his daughter's plantation, Corona, which had been on the promontory east of the river's main channel, found itself on a new island—later named Centennial Island—on the *west* side of the channel. The erosion and shifting of property boundaries sparked years of litigation between plantation owners and also between the states of Arkansas and Tennessee, and before long, criminal elements took advantage of the jurisdictional confusion. By the early 1900s, Island 37, especially, now more or less attached to Arkansas with the silting up of the old river channel, became a harbor for bootleggers, notorious for its "blind tigers," as the bootleggers' dens were called. Though Tipton County, Tennessee, claimed jurisdiction, it was the Arkansas state militia that finally cleaned out the island in 1915, in a raid that killed the sheriff of Mississippi County, Arkansas, and several of the bootleggers. In 1918, the U.S. Supreme Court ruled that Island 37 and Centennial Island were part of Tennessee.

Today, the old river channels have completely silted in except in times of extreme high water, leaving the land connected to Arkansas. Children of the few families living in these Tennessee lands on the west bank of the Mississippi attend school in Arkansas with a special act of the Tennessee legislature to pay their share in lieu of property taxes to the State of Arkansas.

ISLAND 40

Island 40 Road east of Clarkedale, Arkansas

Closer to the Hernando de Soto Bridge is an island known as Island 40—another part of Tennessee stranded on the west bank—that was once home to a large collection of shantyboats. Shantyboats were crude, homemade shacks or houses on barges built by fisherfolk, flood refugees or families who simply had fallen on hard times; the houseboats were a low-cost alternative to life on land. With a steep decline in farm prices following World War I, many farmers found themselves trapped into sharecropping and the crop lien system, which kept them in perpetual debt. Shantyboat life was an appealing alternative: once you had a boat, you could live rent-free on any river or creek, with the freedom to find opportunity wherever it called. Shantyboat families typically sold fish, did odd jobs or hired themselves out for part-time farm labor. By the 1930s, with the onset of the Great Depression, Island 40's shantyboat community rivaled that of many big-city Hoovervilles. Like its urban counterparts, the community at Island 40 largely disappeared with the onset of World War II.

2

MEMPHIS BEFORE MEMPHIS

Recorded history of Memphis begins with the arrival in the area of Spanish explorer Hernando de Soto in 1541, though people had been living here, of course, for thousands of years. The first known inhabitants of West Tennessee, the so-called Paleo Indians, arrived about 12,000 BCE, following migrating herds of Ice Age animals like the mastodon. Not much is known of them, nor of the Archaic Indians who followed, but around 1,000 BCE, the Woodland Culture—a farming people—developed out of the Archaic. They lived in semipermanent settlements and developed vast trade networks that stretched all the way from the Gulf Coast to the Great Lakes and beyond the Mississippi River. They created pottery—some of it startlingly beautiful—and built burial mounds for their dead. By 1000 CE, they had developed a highly complex, stratified culture known as the Mississippian Culture. The Mississippians built bustling, fortified, permanent cities, some with vast mound complexes, and tended large fields of maize, beans and squash. The mounds they built were used primarily for ceremonies and for residences of high-ranking officials, although some were used as burial chambers.

At the time of the de Soto expedition, this stretch of the Mississippi River Valley was one of the most densely populated areas in all of North America. In the Mid-South area, there were two large, rival chiefdoms: the Casqui, centered on the Parkin settlement, near modern Parkin, Arkansas; and the Pacaha, centered near modern Turrel, Arkansas. Little is known of their rich and complex history, but the surviving narratives of Hernando de Soto's expedition indicate that the Casqui and the Pacaha had been at war for generations before the arrival of the Spanish in 1541.

De Soto is said to have been unimpressed with the great Mississippi River, finding it yet another obstacle in his futile three-year quest for gold. He crossed the river somewhere in the vicinity of the future site of Memphis—no one knows exactly where—and headed west and south into Arkansas and Louisiana, but early in 1542, he turned back toward the Mississippi. Soon after, de Soto took ill with a fever and died in May 1542. He had encouraged natives to think of him as an immortal "son of the Sun," so to conceal his death his men secretly sank his body in the middle of the river at night.

After de Soto, the next historical records we have are from an expedition by Father Jacques Marquette and fur trader Louis Joliet down the river in 1673, some 130 years later. By then, the Mississippian people—done in by disease, drought and famine—had abandoned the bluffs to the Chickasaw. Other French explorers followed Marquette, including La Salle in 1682. To them, the river was no obstacle but rather a highway connecting lands far to the north—rich in furs—with an outlet to the sea. They envisioned a great colony stretching from Canada to the Gulf of Mexico; near the mouth of the river they founded a settlement called La Nouvelle–Orleans and worked their way north along the great river highway, securing their new claim. A fort was built on the bluffs, but it was abandoned by 1740.

In 1763, England emerged victorious in a global war with France, known in North America as the French and Indian War. The resulting Treaty of Paris divided North America down the middle: French claims to land west of the Mississippi River were granted to Spain; those east of the river were granted to England. But neither Britain nor Spain occupied the land; it remained the home of the Chickasaw.

It would not be theirs much longer. Another treaty signed in Paris, this one between Britain and the newly independent United States of America, ceded English claims east of the Mississippi to the Americans. American traders began to appear among the Chickasaw, and suddenly, men in North Carolina were speculating in title to lands they had never seen along the Mississippi. Spain thought it best to make something of its holdings in the Mississippi Valley before the Americans, teeming steadily over the mountains from the Atlantic coast, could effectively grab it. In a preemptive move, the Spanish sent Lieutenant Governor Manuel Gayoso to purchase land from the Chickasaw in 1795. In exchange for food, shirts, brandy and firearms, the Chickasaw sold a small strip of land along the bluffs near the confluence of the Mississippi and Wolf Rivers; the next day, Spanish soldiers started clearing brush and trees for the construction of Fort San Fernando de las Barrancas. Six months later, though, in yet another treaty signed in a faraway land, Spain formally ceded all claims to the eastern Mississippi Valley above the thirty-first parallel to the Americans. Governor Gayoso thought the treaty was a mistake and for two years refused to evacuate the fort, hoping his superiors would change their minds. In 1797, he finally gave up, burned the fort and moved to the west bank of the river.

Several months later, the Americans arrived and erected a small stockade on the site of the old Spanish fort, naming it Fort Adams in honor of the president. Later renamed Fort Pike, it was moved in 1798 to a better site farther south atop the ruins of the old French fort. By this time, a motley collection of settlers made their homes around the frontier outpost. They were unaware that, even then, a lawyer and two military heroes in Nashville had big plans for the bluffs.

CHICKASAW HERITAGE PARK

351 Metal Museum Drive

Chickasaw Heritage Park features the remains of a large prehistoric Native American settlement built on the bluffs not by the Chickasaw but by their probable ancestors, the prehistoric Mississippian Culture, sometime around 1000 CE. The site once contained as many as seven mounds of various sizes, though only the two largest remain today.

Chickasaw Heritage Park. *Author photo.*

It is thought that the settlement at Chickasaw Heritage Park was the major ceremonial center for a province the Spanish called Quizquiz, a collection of close to two dozen settlements inhabited by people allied to the Pacaha and led by their chief, Chisca. The settlements include the multiple-mound complexes here and at Chucalissa a short distance south, along with numerous single-mound sites and moundless villages.

The mounds here atop the highest point on the bluffs were later incorporated into both French and early American fortifications discussed later, as well as the massive Civil War Fort Pickering discussed in chapter 4.

CHUCALISSA MUSEUM AND ARCHAEOLOGICAL SITE

T.O. Fuller State Park

Chucalissa is another prehistoric American Indian village site and mound complex built by the Mississippian Culture. Occupied at various times between 1000 and 1500 CE, the town center features two large mounds and a large central plaza. The plaza was used for various ceremonial purposes as well as games of stickball, a rough-and-tumble team sport similar to lacrosse that was known as "the little brother of war." Houses had mud-plastered walls and thatched roofs, and while the chief's house atop the main platform mound was comparatively large—nearly fifty feet square, with interior posts as roof supports—most were small but snug, warm in the winter and cool in the summer. The settlement seems to have been abandoned sometime before de Soto's arrival, but it is estimated that it once contained one thousand inhabitants.

The prehistoric village was discovered during the construction of T.O. Fuller State Park by the Civilian Conservation Corps in 1938, and it was given the name Chucalissa (which means "abandoned house" in the Choctaw language) at that time. The site is operated by the University of Memphis and, in addition to the prehistoric mound complex and a reconstructed house, features an interesting museum with exhibits on Native American history and culture in the region and a hands-on archaeology laboratory—well worth a visit.

FORT SAN FERNANDO/FORT ADAMS, AUCTION SQUARE

A.W. Willis Avenue and North Main Street

Auction Square—one of four squares laid out in the original city plan—is at the probable site of the Spanish fort San Fernando de las Barrancas (St. Ferdinand of the Bluffs). Built in 1795, it was dismantled and abandoned just two years later after Spain ceded to the United States all claims to lands east of the Mississippi River and north of the thirty-first parallel. In 1797, it was also briefly the site of an early American fort, Fort Adams (later renamed Fort Pike).

Auction Square was a focal point of commerce in the city's early years and was the site of the city's first food market. Contrary to some local lore, slaves were never auctioned here; the large block in the middle of the park dates from 1924 and was presented as a gift from the Colonial Dames of America to mark—erroneously—the site where Hernando de Soto first viewed the Mississippi River. Although Memphis was a major slave trading center, slaves were not sold at public auction but instead sold by individual dealers at their own establishments, many of which were located on Adams Avenue near the current site of the courthouse.

FORT ASSUMPTION/FORT PICKERING

351 Metal Museum Drive

In 1739, a French fortification known as Fort De L'Assomption (Fort Assumption) was built here atop the bluffs in the area of today's Chickasaw Heritage Park. The French, from their settlement of New Orleans and their fur trading posts in the Great Lakes region, claimed the entire Mississippi Valley but came into sharp conflict with the Chickasaw, who had other ideas. Of particular concern to the French was the Chickasaw blockade of river traffic at the site of present-day Memphis. French governor Jean-Baptiste Le Moyne, Sieur de Bienville, led a number of unsuccessful campaigns to subdue the Chickasaw between 1721 and 1736 and, finally, in 1739, sailed upriver to rid himself of the Chickasaw menace once and for all. He brought a large force of over one thousand men with heavy artillery and built a strong, star-shaped fort—three bastions facing the land, and two facing the river—for both defense and as a base of operations. He soon found he was unable to transport his artillery through the trackless wilderness and,

Indian Mounds, Chickasaw Heritage Park. *Courtesy of Memphis and Shelby County Room, Memphis Public Library and Information Center.*

in any event, had trouble even finding the Chickasaw; the Chickasaw, for their part, wisely avoided open battle and played a waiting game, harassing the French with small guerrilla raids before melting back into the forest. The Chickasaw strategy paid off: in less than a year, the French, severely weakened from weather, disease, desertion and drunkenness, abandoned the fort and retreated back downriver.

In 1801, a small American fort, Fort Pickering, was built on this site. The first commander of Fort Pickering was Captain Zebulon Pike (father of the famous Rocky Mountain explorer). In 1809, he was replaced by Lieutenant Zachary Taylor, who became the twelfth president forty years later. Meriwether Lewis—of Lewis and Clark fame—was also briefly commander of the garrison at Fort Pickering, the first time the young army officer held the responsibilities of command.

The fort fell into disuse after the Louisiana Purchase when the Mississippi River was no longer the western border of the country. By 1813, all that remained was a corporal and less than a dozen soldiers. It was later completely abandoned, though the tiny settlement around the fort continued to grow and, by the 1840s, had developed into a rival for Memphis. The fort was later revived and greatly expanded in the Civil War (see chapter 4).

3

THE RISE OF MEMPHIS, 1819-1860

The founders had grand plans for the city. Streets were laid out with four public squares and a promenade along the bluffs, although it would take some years for the plans to be fully realized. Starting in 1819, the city took shape around Auction Square, close to the original river landing and near where the Pyramid stands today. Marcus Winchester, son of founder James Winchester, became the city's first mayor and opened the first store, on the corner of Front Street and Jackson Avenue. Irishman Paddy Meagher opened a store and drinking establishment known as the Bell Tavern for the bell he hung in front on the east side of Front Street north of Overton Avenue. The Bell Tavern, frequented by the likes of Sam Houston and Davy Crockett on their travels, became legendary. It stood for nearly one hundred years—at various times a tavern, gambling den, store, church and warehouse—before being razed in 1918. Winchester's store, the city's first cotton gin, courthouse, bank and newspaper office, the market buildings and the city's earliest houses—many built from wood salvaged from abandoned flatboats—are likewise gone, swept away by the march of time and progress.

In 1826, Memphis was officially incorporated as a city, at the time having five hundred residents. By then, it had earned a reputation as a tough river town, a favorite port for flatboat men floating goods down river to New Orleans. In 1826, the first cotton bales arrived by wagon for transshipment down the river, and the city's cotton market was born. By the 1830s, Memphis was an important commercial center, with numerous rivals. The two closest—South Memphis, immediately to the south of the founders' land, and Fort Pickering, a community that grew up in the neighborhood of the now abandoned fort—were simply annexed by Memphis as the city grew. The others—Raleigh to the east, and Randolph on the Second Chickasaw Bluffs to the north—took longer to vanquish.

Over the next few decades, the city gained momentum with an influx of Irish and German immigrants escaping famine and political strife. The immigrants established new businesses, provided labor, built churches and introduced culture; from 1850 to 1860, Memphis was the fastest-growing city in the country, outstripping Brooklyn and Chicago. The Memphis and Charleston Railroad, completed in 1856, connected the East Coast and the Mississippi River for the first time, and Memphis boomed as a commercial distribution center. For better or worse, two commodities shaped the city's economy, created the fortunes on which the city was built and colored much of its subsequent history: cotton and slaves.

COTTON ROW

Front Street between Gayoso and Jefferson Avenues

Memphis is a city built on cotton.

In Tennessee, large-scale production of cotton began in the 1820s as the land between the Tennessee and Mississippi Rivers was opened up after the Chickasaw Cession. The "white gold" soon became the undisputed king here in the southwestern portion of the state, where the deep, rich soil of the Mississippi delta extended up into Shelby, Fayette, Hardeman, Haywood and Madison Counties.

By the time of the Civil War, cotton was far and away the nation's most valuable commodity, accounting for half the value of all U.S. exports. The South grew two-thirds of all the commercially grown cotton in the entire world, and a lot of it came through Memphis. By 1860, Memphis had become the largest inland cotton market in the world and a headquarters for cotton factors, the financial intermediaries who provided planters with operating capital and marketed the crop.

The city was full of businesses connected to cotton: sellers and shippers' offices, storage and compress facilities, insurance companies, wholesale

Front Street, 1890s. *Courtesy of Memphis and Shelby County Room, Memphis Public Library and Information Center.*

grocers, dry goods stores, seed merchants, hotels and bars all grew up around Cotton Row, as Front Street was called between Gayoso and Jefferson Avenues. The busy season was October through January. Heavy bales were loaded onto mule wagons at the riverfront and hauled up the bluff to the merchants' offices on Cotton Row for classification, and long burlap "snakes" of cotton were piled on the sidewalks. Often there were so many white tufts floating through the air that it looked like snow.

Merchants classed cotton according to its grade, staple and color in preparation for offering the bales for sale. There are nine grades, seven colors and seventeen staples of cotton, making over one thousand possible classifications. Classification was as much art as science, and the ritual of the classification process varied considerably depending on the personalities involved. Fortunes could be made or lost depending on a merchant's judgment, but by tradition, sales were closed with a simple handshake.

The buildings of Cotton Row were constructed mostly between 1848 and 1928. You can tell an old cotton building by its slightly wider ground-floor entrance (to facilitate moving bales in and out) and the large windows and north-facing skylights on the top floor, where the visual work of classing took place. The block of unpretentious, utilitarian buildings on the east side of Front Street between Union and General Washburn's Escape Alley is a good example of Cotton Row architecture.

Cotton is still a major commodity in the mid-South—within 150 miles of Memphis, there are typically more than one million acres of land under cotton cultivation—but progress and modernization have eliminated the need for centers such as old Cotton Row.

MONROE AND COURT STREETS

The streets running down to the river on either side of Fourth Bluff Park retain an interesting feature from the nineteenth century. The streets are eighty feet wide—double the width of ordinary city streets—to allow mule teams to zigzag up the steep grade with heavy loads of cotton.

Mule wagon. *Courtesy of Memphis and Shelby County Room, Memphis Public Library and Information Center.*

CALVARY EPISCOPAL CHURCH

102 North Second Street

Calvary Episcopal Church. *Author photo.*

Episcopal services were first held on a flatboat on the river beginning in 1832, but ten years later, the congregation purchased this lot on the corner of Second and Adams. Construction began in 1843 on a design by the congregation's minister, Reverend Philip Alston, who also was an amateur architect. The roof collapsed four years later—Alston was, after all, an amateur—but other than the addition of the tower in 1848 and an addition to the east in 1881, the steep-pitched building remains Alston's basic design. It is the oldest public building still standing in Memphis.

Italian immigrant Philip Flavio was the church organist throughout the 1840s and held popular concerts here in the 1840s and '50s. Known as one of the most versatile and entertaining musicians of his day—perhaps the first "star" on the Memphis music scene—he opened the city's first retail music store on Main Street and offered lessons, as well, laying the foundations of the city's strong musical tradition.

EUGENE MAGEVNEY HOUSE

198 Adams Avenue

This is the oldest home still standing in downtown Memphis, built in 1833 by Irish immigrant Eugene Magevney. It is a good example of the kind of modest, middle-class homes that were common in this part of the city in the middle of the nineteenth century—a simple structure with a large kitchen garden in the rear where the family would grow their own vegetables and herbs.

Magevney studied to be a priest in Ireland but changed his mind and became a schoolteacher instead. In 1828, he immigrated to the United

Eugene Magevney House. *Author photo.*

States and settled in Memphis in 1833. He ran one of the city's first private schools and became a community leader; he served as an alderman and, in 1848, led the fight to establish the city's first public schools.

In 1839, the first Catholic Mass was celebrated here in this house, where the first marriage (his own) and the first baptism (his daughter, Mary) were also celebrated. Magevney was also one of those responsible for the founding of St. Peter's Catholic Church, located next door.

The house was owned by the Magevney family until the 1940s, when it was donated to the city. It is currently open for tours on the first Saturday of every month.

TRAIL OF TEARS

State Route 14 and 717 Island Drive

In 1830, Congress passed the Indian Removal Act, which gave the federal government the power to convince—or coerce—native tribes east of the Mississippi River to exchange their ancestral lands for new lands to the west, in what is today Oklahoma. So began a series of forced relocations of over sixty thousand people from the Choctaw, Creek, Chickasaw, Cherokee and Seminole Nations from Georgia, Tennessee, Alabama, North Carolina and Florida. The "Trail of Tears," as the difficult, and often deadly, marches came to be described, was actually a series of forced relocations engineered by President Andrew Jackson through treaties with the individual tribes.

In the winter of 1831, the Choctaw became the first nation to be expelled from their lands. The forced relocation—without any food, supplies or other help from the government—resulted in the death of thousands along the way. It was, one Choctaw leader said, a "trail of tears and death." In December 1831, the tribe, moving west on the stage road through Bartlett and Raleigh (modern-day State Route 14), arrived in Memphis, where they hoped to cross by boat to Arkansas. The exact location of their departure is unknown. It was likely in the vicinity of where the Pyramid stands today, though a historical marker has been placed on the Mud Island riverbank near the intersection of A.W. Willis Avenue and Island Drive where the view more closely approximates what the Choctaw, and later the Chickasaw and Cherokee, saw from the east bank of the river. As chance would have it, the French writer Alexis de Tocqueville, while on a nine-month tour of the country that resulted in his famed book *Democracy in America*, was in Memphis at the time and recorded their plight:

> At the end of the year 1831, whilst I was on the left bank of the Mississippi at a place named by Europeans, Memphis, there arrived a numerous band of Choctaws.... These savages had left their country, and were endeavoring to gain the right bank of the Mississippi, where they hoped to find an asylum which had been promised them by the American government.
>
> It was then the middle of winter, and the cold was unusually severe; the snow had frozen hard upon the ground, and the river was drifting huge masses of ice. The Indians had their families with them; and they brought in their train the wounded and sick, with children newly born, and old men upon the verge of death. They possessed neither tents nor wagons, but only their arms and some provisions.
>
> I saw them embark to pass the mighty river, and never will that solemn spectacle fade from my remembrance. No cry, no sob was heard amongst the assembled crowd; all were silent. Their calamities were of ancient date, and they knew them to be irremediable. The Indians had all stepped into the bark which was to carry them across, but their dogs remained

upon the bank. As soon as these animals perceived that their masters were finally leaving the shore, they set up a dismal howl, and, plunging all together into the icy waters of the Mississippi, they swam after the boat.

Removal of the Chickasaws, Creeks, Seminoles and Cherokees continued over the next decade. The Chickasaw and many of the Cherokee people moved overland through Memphis in 1832 and 1838, respectively, while other large groups of Cherokee passed through Memphis on a water route down the Mississippi River.

ELMWOOD CEMETERY

824 South Dudley Street

Elmwood Cemetery was founded in 1852 as a garden cemetery on the outskirts of the city. In the mid-nineteenth century, as Memphis grew in population and physically expanded, burial grounds downtown—Winchester Cemetery in the north and Morris Cemetery in the south—were becoming crowded and considered a hindrance to business expansion. A spacious, rural, park-like area was thought to be both healthier as well as more consoling to family and loved ones, a place where the living could commune with nature as a way of finding life in death. To this end, a Cemetery Association was formed and forty acres of wooded rolling hills purchased two miles outside the city limits; an additional forty acres was added after the Civil War.

The name Elmwood was chosen out of a hat full of names in 1852. The Cemetery Association was said to be pleased with the name, although it then had to scramble to order elm trees from New York to plant among the native oaks and magnolias. Entrance to the cemetery is over the high-arched Morgan Bridge, built in 1903. Immediately to the left upon crossing the bridge is the cemetery office, known as the Phillips Cottage, built in 1866, a beautiful example of Victorian carpenter Gothic architecture. The bell beside the cottage has rung at every processional since its placement at the cemetery entrance in the early 1870s.

The first burial was in 1853, of a Mrs. R.B. Berry. Today, over seventy-five thousand people are buried in Elmwood from all walks of life, including politicians, madams, bankers, blues singers, educators, outlaws, millionaires and paupers. Since its earliest days, the cemetery has been inclusive; there are whites and blacks, Irish, Chinese, German, Greek and Mexican immigrants

Elmwood Cemetery.
Author photo.

as well as those of Catholic, Protestant, Jewish and Muslim faiths. It is the final resting place of four U.S. senators, twenty-two mayors of Memphis, two Tennessee governors and veterans of every American war since the Revolution. Over one thousand Confederate veterans are buried in lots donated by the Cemetery Association (the last interment was in 1940); some seven hundred Union soldiers were buried here also, although most were moved to the Memphis National Cemetery in 1866. Annie Cook, a well-known madam who opened her downtown brothel as a makeshift infirmary and died tending the sick during the yellow fever epidemic of 1878, lies near thousands of anonymous fever victims in unmarked graves. The cemetery is also the final resting place of such prominent citizens as E.H. Crump, Robert Church Sr. and historian and writer Shelby Foote.

A one-hour driving tour of the cemetery is available from the office, providing an excellent background on Elmwood's interesting collection of monuments and the stories of those laid to rest here.

BETTIS FAMILY CEMETERY

1620 Madison Avenue

Tucked away behind a low brick wall behind a grocery store parking lot and a Home Depot store is Memphis's oldest surviving cemetery, the Bettis family plot. Tillman Bettis was one of the early settlers of Shelby County, arriving from South Carolina soon after the treaty with the Chickasaw in 1818. Given that several of his brothers continued on to Texas, it is likely that was Bettis's plan as well, but hearing that good land had just become available after the treaty, Bettis and his wife and family elected to stay.

They cleared one of the larger farms in the area in those early days, running south from what is now Poplar Avenue to Union Avenue, and east and west between McNeil and Cooper Streets. The cemetery is all that remains of the Bettis farm. It is likely the house and barns stood nearby, and that the cemetery was originally the garden.

By 1829, Tillman Bettis was one of the leading men in the county and active in its political leadership. One early history of Memphis described him as "rather on the free-and-easy order, fond of his glass, his friends and a good joke; took the world easy and seemed to care but little about the opinions of others."

Bettis died in 1854. He had nine children with his first wife, Sally Carr; their fifth child, Mary Jane, born in 1819, is said to be the first child born in Shelby County. Tillman remarried after Sally Carr's death in 1826 and had an additional seven children with his second wife, also named Sally.

The cemetery contains a shaft in memorial to Tillman and his first wife as well as eight other headstones and slabs, only a few of which are legible. It is believed that there are more graves than markers and that there are additional bodies buried even outside the enclosure.

4

THE CIVIL WAR, 1861-1865

Memphis was a boomtown in the 1850s: in 1859 alone, more than 1,400 new buildings were erected, and even more were begun in 1860. But the city's meteoric rise as one of the South's preeminent cities was brought to an abrupt halt by the Civil War.

In the beginning, Memphis did not favor secession; in fact, some Southerners even accused it of being a Unionist stronghold. While much of Memphis's prosperity was tied to cotton, and while many of the West Tennessee planters were hotly in favor of secession, the city's economic ties to the Yankee merchants of St. Louis, Cincinnati and the upper Mississippi Valley were just as strong. In an article in October 1860, just a few weeks before the presidential election, the *Memphis Appeal* stated there was no reason for secession; even if Lincoln were to win, "Memphis will gain both wealth and population from any civil commotion arising south of us, and we are satisfied that there was never a time when investments here will prove more profitable than those of today."

In the four-way presidential election of 1860, Shelby County voted overwhelmingly—eight to one—for two candidates, Stephen Douglas and John Bell, who favored compromise on the slavery issue while remaining in the Union; Southern Democrat John Breckinridge, a vocal proponent of secession and states' rights, finished a far distant third. (Abraham Lincoln wasn't even on the ballot in Tennessee.) But the following February, when Tennessee held a statewide referendum on secession, Shelby County's support for the Union had lost some steam, and by April, as passions and emotions ran high with the firing on Fort Sumter and Lincoln's call for troops, public opinion changed drastically. In June 1861, Shelby County ratified secession nearly unanimously, with only five votes against.

In the Confederate army's initial call for volunteers, more than 3,800 Memphians enlisted, a higher percentage of the population than in any other major city in the country, North or South.

The city was coveted by both North and South; the river and the city's extensive rail network made it an important supply depot. At dawn on June 6, 1862, thousands of the city's residents lined the bluffs above the river to watch the Confederate fleet of "cottonclads" battle a Union naval force that steamed out of the morning mist. By noon it was all over, and Yankee soldiers in blue occupied the city.

Spared the destruction of other Southern cities, Memphis suffered comparatively little under Union occupation. In many ways, it was business as usual. The city's merchants were conveniently placed middlemen between North and South, selling cotton and food to the Union and smuggling gunpowder, shoes and medicine on the black market to the Confederates. The war did bring profound change to Memphis, however: freed slaves fled by the thousands to the city and the freedmen's camps established here by Union authorities, laying the groundwork for dramatic cultural changes in the years to come.

Arguably the city's most significant contribution to the war was Nathan Bedford Forrest. Both celebrated and reviled, Forrest is one of the more controversial figures of the Civil War era. Born to a poor family in Chapel Hill, Tennessee, and largely uneducated, he moved to Memphis and amassed a fortune prior to the Civil War in cotton, real estate and the slave trade. He was one of the city's most prominent slave traders and operated a large slave yard on Adams Avenue between Second and Third Streets. In 1858, he was elected as a city alderman, serving three terms.

Forrest enlisted in the Confederate army as a private but, due to his wealth and status, was given the rank of lieutenant colonel and invited to lead a cavalry regiment, a role he seemed born to fill. He established a reputation for boldness and personal bravery in the early battles of Fort Donelson and Shiloh, but it was his raids and tactical campaigns in Middle and West Tennessee that played havoc with the Union army throughout the entire conflict. General Sherman considered him the most dangerous man in the Confederacy, reportedly saying that he should "be hunted down and killed if it costs 10,000 lives and bankrupts the treasury." Forrest was also most notoriously the commander of the

Confederate forces at the 1864 Battle of Fort Pillow, where, by some accounts he ordered—or turned a blind eye to—the slaughter of African American troops attempting to surrender.

After the war, Forrest returned to Memphis and engaged in several business ventures. He also became the first grand wizard of the Ku Klux Klan. He subsequently resigned and ordered the disbanding of the organization and, late in life, gave a speech at the Memphis Fairgrounds to a black audience and called for understanding and cooperation between the races.

In 1904—twenty-seven years after his death—he was honored with a heroic equestrian statue in an eight-acre park named for him on Union Avenue, and he and his wife were disinterred from Elmwood Cemetery and reburied there. The park—long a flashpoint of racial controversy—was renamed Health Sciences Park in 2013, and four years later, the statue was removed. (At the same time, the city also removed a statue of Confederate president Jefferson Davis from a park on Front Street.) At this writing, Forrest and his wife are still buried in the park, although it seems likely they will ultimately return to Elmwood Cemetery.

HOWARD'S ROW

Union Avenue between Riverside Drive and Front Street

This row of buildings, built by Wardlow Howard in 1848 and originally known as "Howard's Row," is one of the oldest in Memphis and was an early commercial center where you could buy almost anything—including slaves.

Memphis, along with Savannah and New Orleans, was one of the largest slave markets in the entire country. Most of the city's slave firms, including Hill and Forrest (co-owned by Nathan Bedford Forrest), were located on Adams Avenue east of Main Street. But one firm, Bolton & Dickens, was here at Howard's Row, close to the river landing.

Bolton & Dickens was one of the largest slave firms in the entire South, a sophisticated and complex operation with branch offices in New Orleans, Vicksburg, Mobile, Richmond and Lexington, Kentucky. The firm's agents bought slaves in the Upper South and sold them in the Deep South, using Memphis as a convenient way station between the two regions. According to one Tennessee newspaper, at their peak "the Boltons were worth nearly $1 million." The firm was dissolved in 1858

Howard's Row. *Author photo.*

after Isaac Bolton murdered a man in his Howard's Row establishment, another slave dealer who had sold him a free man. Bolton was arrested and brought to trial; he was acquitted, but he subsequently took the expenses of the trial (which included nearly $100,000 in bribes to witnesses and jurors) out of the firm's profits, plunging the Bolton and Dickens families into a bitter, bloody feud that killed twelve men over the next thirteen years.

The building at 47 Union Avenue also served as a hospital during the Civil War, one of many buildings in the city put to such use.

HUNT-PHELAN HOUSE

533 Beale Street

The Hunt-Phelan House is one of the oldest and most historic houses in Memphis. Designed by Robert Mills, architect of the Washington Monument and the U.S. Treasury Building in Washington, D.C., it was completed in 1842. It has hosted more American presidents—Andrew Jackson, Martin Van Buren, Andrew Johnson and Grover Cleveland, as well as Confederate president Jefferson Davis—than any other place in Memphis except the Peabody Hotel.

During the Civil War, it was the residence of William Richardson Hunt. Hunt, son of a doctor in Washington, Georgia, graduated from the University of Virginia and became a Mississippi planter before moving to Memphis in

Hunt-Phelan House. *Author photo.*

1852. When Tennessee seceded and organized its provisional army, Hunt was made a lieutenant colonel in charge of establishing an arsenal in Memphis, "a duty for which he was peculiarly fitted by his knowledge of chemistry and superior administrative ability," in the words of one Confederate history. Hunt's efforts made Memphis one of the leading cannon producers in the South before the city fell to the Union army.

The house briefly served as headquarters for Union general Ulysses S. Grant, who planned the Vicksburg campaign in the home's mahogany-paneled library. Afterward, the house and grounds served as a hospital; in 1864 alone, more than nineteen thousand soldiers received treatment here. More importantly, a small structure behind the gardens at the rear of the house became the site of one of the first Freedmen's Bureau schools for African Americans. Union occupation of the city and the presence of the Freedmen's Bureau contributed greatly to the quadrupling of the city's African American population during the war; the location of a freedmen's school here cemented Beale Street and South Memphis as the center of the city's burgeoning black community.

The Hunts regained possession of the house after the war. Family legend has it that a household slave had hidden gold from the Yankees by burying it on the property but then died of a fever; efforts to find the treasure ever since have been unsuccessful.

Colonel and Sarah Hunt's daughter Julia married George Phelan in 1872, and the house remained in the Phelan family until 1993. By then, it was the last remaining of the many fine mansions that lined the once fashionable eastern end of Beale Street. It is now a popular wedding and event venue.

BUST OF JACKSON

Shelby County Courthouse, 140 Adams Avenue

In 1859, the city installed, with great fanfare, a bust of Andrew Jackson in the middle of Court Square. It was sculpted by James Frazee, on a pedestal bearing Jackson's famous words "The Federal Union—It Must and Shall Be Preserved." The phrase, coming from Jackson's response to the South Carolina secession crisis of 1832, may have seemed an odd or unusual choice for a southern city in 1859 in the midst of another, more serious, secession crisis. In a dedicatory address, though, the Reverend Andrew Ewing of the Second Presbyterian Church emphasized that the South wished to preserve a union where all of the states were unquestionably equal and refrained from intermeddling in one another's affairs. Nonetheless, the pedestal was heavily defaced by a Southern sympathizer after Union occupation of the city and the bust was removed from public display until 1921, when it found a home in the Shelby County Courthouse, where it is currently on display.

BATTLE OF MEMPHIS

Mississippi River, June 6, 1862

Thousands of Memphians crowded the bluffs—including what would later become Fourth Bluff Park—in the early morning hours of June 6, 1862, to watch the Confederate River Defense Fleet's last-ditch effort to save the city from advancing Union forces. For Southerners, it was not a happy day.

The Union army and navy had been steadily pushing their way down the Mississippi River in the early months of 1862. After Northern victories at Shiloh in April and Corinth on May 30, it was apparent that the Confederates could no longer defend West Tennessee; indeed, on June 4, General Braxton Bragg ordered the small detachment of troops in Memphis and the surrounding area to abandon the city. Only the river defense fleet, such as it was, remained. The fleet, under the command of steamboat captain John Montgomery, gave serious thought to abandoning the city, too, and steaming to Vicksburg, but they discovered they didn't have enough coal to make the trip. Rather than simply scuttle their boats, they decided to stick it out and fight.

Just a few weeks earlier, Captain Montgomery had led the fleet in a minor but uplifting victory when they managed to surprise the Northerners at Plum Point, about forty miles upstream, and sank two Union gunboats with no loss of their own. So it was with some confidence that they sallied out from the cobblestone landing to do battle.

They were eight vessels in all, peacetime steamboats that had been hastily converted to military use by the addition of a few cannons and—in a move that captured the public imagination—hulls and bulkheads reinforced by stacked cotton bales. These so-called "cottonclads" expected to face five Union ironclad gunboats, only to find that the Union fleet now also contained four speedy, maneuverable rams.

The battle began with the Confederate flotilla steaming upstream in line abreast toward the Union vessels, which in turn were lined up stern first, firing their rear guns at the approaching Southerners. Then one of the Union rams steamed through the line, slammed one Confederate boat and turned to strike another. A general melee ensued.

Accounts of the battle differ widely, but all agree on the outcome: after ninety minutes, one Union boat was slightly damaged, while seven of the eight Confederate boats were run aground, disabled or sinking fast into the brown water of the Mississippi. The eighth was fortunate to escape downriver.

After the battle, a small detachment of Union troops landed and marched up the bluff.

The mayor of Memphis refused to say he was "surrendering" the city. However, he did say that he would acquiesce in its occupation. A crowd of people followed the Union soldiers to the post office on the corner of Adams Avenue and Third Street (B.B. King Boulevard, today) to raise the flag. The soldiers were led inside the building and up the stairs, through a trap door and onto the roof, and hoisted the flag to a chorus of boos from the crowd below. While they were up there, someone in the crowd fired a pistol at them (and missed); it was the only act of active resistance by the citizens. When the soldiers turned to go back down, however, they discovered that someone had closed and locked the door, trapping them on the roof. Everyone below got a good laugh, until the Union commander on the river sent word that they had five minutes to let them down, or he'd start bombarding the town. The soldiers were let go, and the city settled in for occupation by the joyless Yankees. The city remained in Union hands for the remainder of the war.

There were 182 Confederate casualties in the river battle and only 1 Union casualty: an officer who was wounded by a stray pistol shot and who later died in the hospital after contracting measles.

FORT PICKERING

351 Metal Museum Drive

Old Fort Pickering, the little frontier fort on the bluffs on the strategic site of the old Indian mounds that was abandoned after the Louisiana Purchase, was brought back to life with the Civil War. The Confederates had neither the time nor the resources to revitalize the site for river defense before surrendering Memphis, but the Union army rebuilt the fort on a grand scale beginning in 1862. The new fort stretched for two miles along the bluff from the mounds in Chickasaw Heritage Park all the way north to Vance Street; it was large enough to accommodate ten thousand men and was designed with some of the most elaborate fortifications of the time. Both of the existing Indian mounds were used as gun batteries: the larger mound was hollowed out and used as a powder magazine. (The entrance to the brick bunker dug into the side of the mound can still be seen from the street.)

After President Lincoln and the War Department authorized the formation of volunteer regiments of African Americans, almost 1,200 African American men enlisted in the Union army at Fort Pickering, making it one of the largest such recruitment sites in the country. The fort was also home to thousands of former slaves who left their plantations and came to work for the Federal forces. Following the war, an African American community grew up nearby.

On May 1, 1866, an altercation just outside the fort between white Memphians resentful of years of military occupation and recently discharged black troops degenerated into a full-scale riot lasting three days; when the smoke cleared, over forty African Americans had been killed, numerous more wounded and over one hundred black homes, churches and schools burned in one of the worst race riots in the country's history.

TOWN OF RANDOLPH

Tipton County, 835 Randolph Road, Drummonds, Tennessee

The town of Randolph was founded in 1823 about thirty miles north of Memphis on the Second Chickasaw Bluff, where the Hatchie River meets the Mississippi. With over twenty commercial establishments by the 1830s, it was at that time the busiest steamboat port in Tennessee, shipping more than twice as much cotton as its southern rival. The flatboat trade still favored the shallow, sandy landing at Memphis, but Memphis was in danger of being left behind in the march of progress; a series of cholera and yellow fever epidemics and an outbreak of dengue fever in Memphis only made Randolph all the more attractive. For a time, it seemed that Randolph, not Memphis, would become the premier city on the bluffs of the Mississippi.

Memphis began to get a leg up on things in the 1840s and '50s by virtue of its good stage roads and a more favorable location for railroads. The death knell for Randolph came during the Civil War. At the beginning of the war, Randolph was the site of two Confederate forts, Fort Wright and

Fort Randolph, on either side of the mouth of the Hatchie River that served as early training camps for Confederate soldiers; Nathan Bedford Forrest, among many others, began his military training there. The Confederates abandoned the forts in 1862, and the posts fell into disuse, but Randolph became the center of roving bands of guerrillas who attacked Union patrols, supply trains and boats traveling past on the river. When the unarmed steamer *Eugene* was fired on in September 1862, the Union commander of Memphis, General William T. Sherman, had enough. He ordered a regiment to "destroy the town, leaving one house to mark the place." It was the beginnings of Sherman's "hard war" approach, an approach he was to greatly expand in his destructive march through Georgia just two years later. As he wrote to General Grant a few weeks after the destruction of Randolph, the local people "cannot be made to love us, but they can be made to fear us."

Though attempts were made to reinhabit the town after the war, Randolph never recovered. Today, all that remains of old Randolph is the hillside powder magazine of Fort Wright (on private property) and, along the river, the faint trace of a path that was once a town thoroughfare.

GENERAL WASHBURN'S ESCAPE ALLEY

South Main Street between Union and Monroe Avenues

The street gets its unique and colorful name from Confederate general Nathan Bedford Forrest's daring raid on August 21, 1864.

A large Union force under the command of General A.J. Smith, some twenty thousand strong, had been sent to find and destroy Forrest's cavalry in the neighborhood of Oxford, Mississippi, sixty miles southwest of Memphis. Forrest, rather than wait to be attacked, left a small force to keep the Union army occupied in Oxford and led the rest of his men in an attack on Memphis. In addition to creating confusion and mayhem, he hoped to free Confederate prisoners and maybe even capture some Union generals quartered in the city, including Major General Cadwallader Washburn, the Union army's commander for west Tennessee, and Major General Stephen Hurlbut, the former west Tennessee commander.

With fewer than 1,500 men (including his younger brothers Captain Bill Forrest and Lieutenant Colonel Jesse Forrest), Forrest's men rode through the night and swooped down on unsuspecting Union troops in Memphis just before dawn. As Bill Forrest rode his horse into the lobby of the Gayoso Hotel on Front Street in search of General Hurlbut, Lieutenant Colonel Jesse Forrest led a party of men to General Washburn's quarters on Union Avenue near Fourth Street. Washburn was awakened by the sounds of Confederate soldiers breaking through the front door and narrowly managed to escape out a back entrance. He fled down this alley—still dressed in his nightshirt—to the river and the safety of Fort Pickering. Forrest's men seized Washburn's uniform, his sword and some papers before withdrawing south down the Hernando Road.

Forrest's plan worked: on receiving frantic messages that Forrest was attacking Memphis, General Smith turned his men around and marched back.

Forrest had Washburn's uniform cleaned and pressed and returned it to him later that day under a flag of truce. Washburn graciously responded by sending to Forrest a fine gray uniform made to measure by Forrest's own prewar Memphis tailor, along with enough gray cloth and buttons and gold lace to make full uniforms for his staff. The last word on the raid, though, belongs to Union general Hurlbut, who grumbled one of the wittier remarks of the war: "They removed me from command because I couldn't keep Forrest out of West Tennessee, but Washburn can't keep him out of his own bedroom!"

SULTANA DISASTER MUSEUM

140 Washington Avenue, Marion, Arkansas

In the early morning hours of April 27, 1865, the steamboat *Sultana* exploded and caught fire in the Mississippi River just a few miles north of Memphis, killing more than 1,700 men in what remains the worst maritime disaster in U.S. history. The men were mostly Union soldiers returning home after the war, many of them recently released from Confederate prison camps in Georgia, Alabama and Mississippi.

The *Sultana* was a 260-foot-long wooden steamboat that regularly transported passengers and freight between St. Louis and New Orleans on the Mississippi River. On a trip upriver in April 1865, the boat put in at Vicksburg to address some issues with its boilers. While in port, the captain, J. Cass Mason, was approached with a proposition to transport Union soldiers, recently released from Confederate prisoner-of-war camps, upriver. At five dollars per enlisted man and ten dollars for each officer, it was an offer he couldn't refuse, and he bribed an army officer to let the *Sultana* take the entire group. The vessel, which had two lifeboats with a total capacity of 76, was certified for 376 passengers and crew; Captain Mason took on more than 2,300 passengers—more than six times the limit—and stopped for more in Natchez and Helena on the way upriver. The passengers were so tightly sandwiched together that many could find no place to sleep; the decks sagged and creaked under the load.

The *Sultana* steamed north up the Mississippi, but the severe overcrowding and fast river current caused by the spring thaw put increased pressure on its newly patched boilers. The boat left the Memphis wharf shortly after midnight on April 26, 1865, and stopped briefly at Hopefield, across the river, to take on more coal. Seven or eight miles upriver, at a little after 3:00 a.m., the overstrained boilers exploded, blowing apart the center of the boat and starting an uncontrollable fire. Those who were not killed immediately were scalded by the boilers, burned in the fire and drowned in the cold and swift river. Estimates put the death toll that night at well over one thousand; more died in the coming days and weeks from burns sustained during the incident.

The Mississippi River has changed course several times since the disaster, and the main channel is now about two miles east of its 1865 position. In 1982, archaeologists discovered what are believed to be the remains of the *Sultana* more than thirty feet under a soybean field near Marion, Arkansas.

For the 150th anniversary of the disaster in 2015, the City of Marion created a museum telling the story of the tragedy; it is certainly worth a visit. The museum has a number of fascinating artifacts, including a box made by a survivor out of a crate that had held the boat's pet alligator; the soldier, Private William Lugenbeal of the 135th Ohio Volunteer Infantry, had used the wooden pen as a raft (after, sadly, killing the alligator).

MEMPHIS NATIONAL CEMETERY

3568 Townes Avenue

Memphis National Cemetery is the final resting place for more than forty thousand veterans from the Civil War to the present day.

After the North captured Memphis in 1862, the Union army took advantage of the city's transportation links and established numerous hospitals in Memphis to care for wounded troops from across the

Memphis National Cemetery.
Author photo.

region. These hospitals, though better staffed and organized than most Civil War facilities, nonetheless had high death rates and created a pressing need for burial space; the dead were initially interred in private cemeteries throughout the Memphis area, including Elmwood Cemetery.

Congress created the first fourteen national cemeteries in 1862 and, by war's end, established sixty more, including the Memphis National Cemetery. The earliest burials here were of casualties who died in the city's hospitals, followed by battlefield reinterments from Tennessee, Kentucky, Arkansas and Mississippi. The cemetery contains the remains of more than eight thousand unknown soldiers, the second most of any national cemetery (after Vicksburg National Cemetery), due to lack of identification and deterioration of the often hastily dug battlefield graves. Notable Civil War burials include Private James Robinson of the Third Michigan Volunteer Cavalry, a Medal of Honor recipient killed in 1864, and over 4,000 U.S. Colored Troops (250 of them unknown), as well as many of those who died in the SS *Sultana* tragedy.

5

DEATH AND REBIRTH, 1865–1908

Memphis—like much of the South—suffered an economic depression in the years immediately following the war, but by 1870, it had largely recovered. At the beginning of the decade, the city was twice the size of its rival, Atlanta, and looked ready to pick right up where it had left things at the beginning of the war. But dark days lay ahead.

In 1873, the city had an outbreak of yellow fever that claimed over two thousand lives. The fever struck again in 1878. Within days, more than half the city had fled, many never to return; of the twenty thousand who remained, more than five thousand died. By the time it was over, the city had permanently lost one-quarter of its population. The city government, noted neither for its honesty nor efficiency even in the best of times, tottered on the edge of bankruptcy. With its tax base suddenly eroded, the city defaulted on its bond payments, and the state legislature repealed the city's charter. Memphis ceased to exist—at least as a corporate entity. Declared a taxing district, Memphis was placed under the control of a state commission, leaving residents little say in local affairs.

To make matters worse, in 1879, the fever struck yet again, and though milder than the previous year (causing only 595 deaths), it lasted longer and did even greater economic damage. It was the last straw for the city's wealthier citizens; many who had the means to move elsewhere turned their back on the city forever. With real estate values crumbling, thousands of its most productive citizens lost, its finances destroyed with no credit available for redevelopment and a reputation as one of the unhealthiest places to live in the country, the city's future looked bleak indeed. There was some serious discussion about abandoning the city altogether as a place unfit to live.

Under a fiscal austerity program and intelligent leadership, however, the city fought its way back. Dr. D.T. Porter, the city's first president of the taxing district, took bold steps to clean the city environment. Though it was not discovered that yellow fever was mosquito-borne until the 1890s, many suspected that the city's poor sanitation was a factor. When Porter learned of a revolutionary new type of sewer system designed by sanitary engineer George Waring Jr., he immediately ordered its adoption in Memphis. Installed by 1880, the Waring System—also sometimes known as the Memphis System—was the first of its kind anywhere in the world and is now commonplace. Porter also hired uniformed city sanitation officers to go house to house to enforce strict new sanitary regulations. These and other measures had the unwitting effect of destroying mosquito breeding grounds in backyard wells and cisterns. The city was never plagued by yellow fever again.

As if to make up for lost time, the city—with its charter restored in 1893—grew rapidly over the next decades. New levees turned swamps into rich farmland, and fortunes were made as lumber was cleared from the land. Steamboat traffic rose to new records, new railroads were built

Cobblestone landing and steamboat *James Lee*. *Courtesy of Memphis and Shelby County Room, Memphis Public Library and Information Center.*

and the Great Bridge, the first to cross the Mississippi below St. Louis, was constructed. Known today as the Frisco Bridge, it made the city one of the nation's leading rail centers.

As business grew, so did the population. Economic opportunity brought migrants from rural areas as well as a new influx of immigrants from abroad; by 1900, Memphis was the third-largest city in the South, with a population for the first time of more than 100,000, eclipsing both Atlanta and Nashville. Starting in the 1890s, a high-rise office building boom began, transforming the city skyline: the Continental Bank Building, completed in 1895, was followed by the Tennessee Trust Building (1907), the Falls Building (1909) and the Exchange Building (1910). Merchant kings, flush with cotton money, erected ostentatious mansions in fashionable neighborhoods on the edge of town and supported new cultural institutions such as the Cossitt Library, the Grand Opera House and the Brooks Museum of Art. New city parks were developed, including beautiful Overton Park, laid out, in part, by the designers of New York City's Central Park. Life became fun again. Racetracks and the city's first amusement parks were built on the outskirts of town, and Sunday afternoons saw crowds of men in bowler hats and women in long skirts roller skating in Forrest Park or enjoying the bandstand and dance pavilion atop the Indian mound at Jackson Mound Park (now Chickasaw Heritage Park). It was a freewheeling time of horse racing, gambling, whiskey and beer, a Gilded Age of opportunity and progress.

COURT SQUARE

North Main Street and Court Avenue

Picturesque Court Square is an oasis of sorts in downtown Memphis. Davy Crockett and Sam Houston lounged in the park on their visits to town, and it has long been a favorite spot for shoppers and office workers to relax. Although Court Square was one of the four public squares laid out in the original city plan (the others were Market, Auction and Exchange), it remained marked only by survey stakes for some years after the city's founding. Despite its name, there never really was a court here. Originally, there was a log cabin near the middle of the square, which at various times served as a church and a storehouse and was only occasionally used as a courthouse. The misnomer is not unique: the city's first court faced Market

Court Square fountain, 1900. *Courtesy of Memphis and Shelby County Room, Memphis Public Library and Information Center.*

Square, a city market was located at Exchange Square and no auctions were ever performed in Auction Square.

In 1858, a campaign was undertaken to beautify the park, which had suffered from the effects of horses, pigs and other free-roaming livestock. A gated iron fence was installed, along with extensive plantings of magnolias, oaks and shrubbery; by 1865, the square's magnolia trees were the pride of Memphis, so much so that the Union army had to place a guard in the park that spring to keep soldiers from climbing the trees and stripping them of their blossoms.

In April 1865, in a gesture of goodwill toward the citizens of Memphis, the Union army's post band began playing concerts in the park every afternoon at five o'clock. The concerts were so popular that other bands appeared for summer concerts, and in 1870, the city council erected a permanent bandstand. Musical concerts have been a permanent fixture in the square since that time.

In the closing days of the Civil War, a young Thomas Edison worked as a telegraph operator in a Western Union office (now gone) located on the north side of the square. Tinkering as always in his spare time, he invented several devices during his time in Memphis, including an automatic telegraph relay system. He also invented a device to electrocute cockroaches: two baited strips of tinfoil glued to the wall above his desk and wired to one of the large batteries that powered the telegraph wires. Cockroaches walked on the strips, and when their legs were on both strips at the same time, the electricity surged through the roaches and killed them in a flash of light and puff of smoke. Word spread of the invention, and so many visitors crowded the telegraph office to watch it in action that his irritated boss made him stop using it.

The fountain was dedicated in 1876 for the centennial of the United States. It is known as the Hebe Fountain for its beautiful reproduction, at the top, of the statue of Hebe, the goddess of youth, by Italian sculptor Antonio Canova. (The original statue is in the Hermitage in St. Petersburg, Russia.) The water in the fountain was originally ten feet deep and once housed both ducks and baby alligators—although presumably not at the same time. During the city's spectacular Mardi Gras celebrations of 1878, the fountain ran with champagne. The fountain was a gift to the city from fifty private donors whose names are carved in the surrounding wall. One of the more interesting names, Madam Vincent, wasn't the proprietress of a brothel but was actually a successful and quite respectable businesswoman, who operated a popular café and several groceries, one of which was located on the northwest corner of the square.

MARTYR'S PARK

Channel 3 Drive off Riverside Drive

Martyr's Park was dedicated in 1972 to commemorate those who died serving others during the city's disastrous yellow fever epidemics of the 1870s. The twenty-foot monument was created by Memphis-area artist Harris Sorelle.

Although Memphis had been exposed to yellow fever in 1828, 1855 and 1867, nothing prepared the city for the devastation the fever brought during the 1870s. An 1873 epidemic claimed two thousand lives in Memphis, a number that constituted at the time the most yellow fever victims in an inland city. In 1878, however, Memphis was forever changed by ten weeks of epidemic. The outbreak came north up the river from New Orleans and ravaged cities, big and small, all along the Mississippi

River. Overall, more than twenty thousand died along the Mississippi River. Memphis was hit most savagely.

No one knew at the time that the disease was spread by mosquitoes; they believed it was caused by bad air arising from marshy or swampy ground. What they did know was that yellow fever meant, in most cases, a horrible death. The first symptoms were chills, nausea, severe pains in the head and back and high fever. After anywhere from a few hours to a few days, the fever subsided. A lucky few slowly recovered and were immune ever after. For the rest, however, the fever would return, and their skin and eyes would turn yellow. Internal bleeding, black vomit and delirium followed. The victims died in agony, filth and stench.

In late July and early August 1878, the city had its first cases of yellow fever, and soon the panic was on. Within ten days of the first reported case, more than twenty-five thousand people fled the city (many never to return) by any means they could manage, with some going to places as far off as St. Louis and Cincinnati. Only about twenty thousand people remained in town, mostly the poor who could not afford to leave and had nowhere to go. In September, there were nearly two hundred deaths a day. Before the end of the epidemic, virtually all who remained would come down with the fever.

Martyr's Park. *Author photo.*

There were a few brave men and women, doctors, nurses and volunteers who stayed in the city to care for the victims, bury the dead and carry on the simple mechanics of living. Among these were the doctors of the Howard Association, a benevolent society organized to aid fever victims, and the city's ministers, priests and nuns who, regardless of the peril, would not turn away from those in the direst need. It is to these brave and charitable souls that the park is dedicated.

ST. MARY'S EPISCOPAL CATHEDRAL

692 Poplar Avenue

St. Mary's began as a mission church, organized by Calvary Episcopal Church in 1857. It became the cathedral church of the Episcopal Diocese of Tennessee—later the West Tennessee Diocese—in 1871.

At the time of the church's founding, the surrounding area was semirural at the eastern edge of the city. The original church was a small, wooden Gothic structure and officially dedicated in 1858. In 1873, St. Mary's School for Girls was opened by a group of Episcopal nuns from the recently formed Sisterhood of St. Mary.

In the yellow fever epidemic of 1878, which ultimately claimed the lives of nearly a quarter of the city's population, the cathedral was turned into an infirmary. The nuns' superior, Sister Constance, traveling at the time the

St. Mary's Episcopal Cathedral. *Courtesy of Memphis and Shelby County Room, Memphis Public Library and Information Center.*

fever hit, returned to Memphis as soon as she heard the news; warned that the church was in the infected zone, Sister Constance nonetheless proceeded directly to the church, where she and other nuns of St. Mary's cared for the sick in the infirmary, sent orphaned children out of the city and took soup and medicine on house calls. Within a month, Constance, three other Episcopal nuns and two Episcopal priests were victims themselves. The cathedral's high altar, dedicated in 1879, memorializes their sacrifice.

Construction of the present English Gothic Revival structure began in 1898 and was completed in 1926. The small chapel on the east side of the cathedral, built in the 1880s, has one of the few wooden Gothic interiors from the nineteenth century remaining in the city. The church hall has interesting exhibits on yellow fever as well as the church's role in the Sanitation Strike of 1968, worth a visit.

TENNESSEE BREWERY

495 Tennessee Street

Built between 1877 and 1890, this ornate, castle-like building was the former home of the Tennessee Brewing Company, at one time the largest brewery in the South. The brewery was originally constructed for the Memphis Brewing Company but was purchased in 1885 by the Tennessee Brewing Company, founded by John Schorr. Schorr, whose family had been brewing beer in Germany for over five hundred years, was a former superintendent in a family brewery in St. Louis and came to Memphis at age twenty-two to try his own hand in the family business. The brewery's formal opening took place on June 7, 1885, when forty thousand glasses of free beer were served to the public.

The brewery took advantage of Memphis's pure artesian water and sank a well on the property to tap into the underground aquifer. Within years, the brewery was so successful that it expanded, adding its own ice plant and keeping a fleet of twenty horse-drawn wagons busy delivering barrels to saloons all over Memphis. By 1908, the brewery had three bottling machines turning out 1,250 pints a day and had more than five hundred employees.

During Prohibition, which came to Tennessee in 1909, a full ten years before becoming national law, the brewery stayed open as the Tennessee Beverage Company, relying on the sales of ice and a drink known as Nib, which stood for "nonintoxicating beverage." When Prohibition was repealed

Tennessee Brewery. *Courtesy of Memphis and Shelby County Room, Memphis Public Library and Information Center.*

in 1933, the brewery switched back to beer, and its Goldcrest label became the most popular beer in Memphis and the region. A million-dollar expansion of the facilities followed in 1948, but increased production costs and stiff competition from national brewers led to slumping sales; the brewery closed its doors in 1954. It has recently been renovated and reopened into apartments and condos.

WOODRUFF-FONTAINE HOUSE

680 Adams Avenue

Unlike its immediate neighbor the James Lee House or the Mallory-Neely House down the street, the Woodruff-Fontaine House was built all at one time. It was designed by Edward Culliatt Jones and his partner, Mathias Baldwin, two of the city's leading architects of the day.

It was built in 1871 for Amos Woodruff, a New Jersey carriage maker who had come to Memphis twenty-five years earlier and had risen to become president of two banks, a railroad company, a cotton compress and a lumber company as well as an alderman and president of the city council. It is said to be haunted by Woodruff's daughter, Mollie, who lost both her firstborn son and her husband to illnesses in the second-floor Rose Room.

In 1883, Woodruff sold the house to Noland Fontaine, president of Hill, Fontaine & Company, at the time the world's third-largest cotton company. The Fontaine family lived here for the next forty-six years. Noland and his wife, Virginia, were famous for their lavish parties, and like the Neelys, moved in the highest circles of Memphis society. They celebrated the opening of the Great Memphis Bridge in 1892 with a reception at the house for more than two thousand guests, among them five state governors. John Philip Sousa is said to have conducted the orchestra at another of their garden soirees, and President Grover Cleveland was entertained here during his Memphis visit in 1887.

The house was used as an art school until the late 1950s. After sitting vacant for a few years, it was rescued by the Association for Preservation of Tennessee Antiquities through a public fund drive and is now open for tours.

Woodruff-Fontaine House. *Author photo.*

JAMES LEE HOUSE

690 Adams Avenue

James Lee House. *Author photo.*

Like the Mallory-Neely House down the street, this house began as a much more modest structure—in this case, a relatively plain two-story farmhouse built in 1848 that fronted onto Orleans Street. William Harsson, a native of Baltimore, was the original owner. One of Harsson's daughters, Sophia, married James Maydwell and lived two doors down at 664 Adams (known today as the Massey House); another of Harsson's daughters, Laura, married Charles Wesley Goyer, who, in 1852, bought this house from his father-in-law. The Goyer family would live here until 1890.

Goyer was a sugar and molasses importer who grew so rich, it is said, that he founded Union Planters Bank just to have some place to keep all of his money. When it was necessary in 1871 to expand the house (the Goyers would eventually have ten children), Goyer hired architects Edward Culliatt Jones and Mathias Baldwin after seeing their work on the Woodruff house next door, and they gave him a very similar building, tower and all, reoriented toward Adams Avenue. Interestingly, the rich effect of the front sandstone façade gives way to stucco or bare brick on the less important side and rear faces of the house.

In 1890, the house was sold to James Lee Jr., son of a steamboat magnate, who moved here from 239 Adams Avenue with his family of ten children. The bell from the riverboat *James Lee* hangs near the side door of the house along Orleans Street.

The house is now a bed-and-breakfast.

MALLORY-NEELY HOUSE

652 Adams Avenue

The Gilded Age in Memphis—an age of elegance, refinement, taste and manners as well as the conspicuous display of wealth and status—had perhaps its crowning embodiment in the Mallory-Neely House. Beautiful Frances "Daisy" Neely—daughter of James Columbus Neely, one of the richest cotton factors in Memphis—and Barton Lee Mallory, a cotton factor and son of a Confederate officer, were at the very pinnacle of the economic, social and political life of Memphis, and their house affords a unique window into the life of the Memphis elite of the era.

The Mallory-Neely House—the grand dame of what is now known as Victorian Village—began as a relatively modest one-story structure, built in 1852 by Isaac Kirtland, a prominent banker. During the Civil War, it was purchased by cotton factor Benjamin Babb, who added a second story before selling it to James Neely in 1883.

It was Neely, a produce dealer and cotton factor, who restyled the house in the 1890s and gave it the look it has to this day. He added the third story and heightened the central tower to get a view all the way to the Mississippi River. Neely also modernized the house, using a newfangled invention

Mallory-Neely House. *Courtesy of Memphis and Shelby County Room, Memphis Public Library and Information Center.*

called window screens—believed to be the first in Memphis—and installing air channels into the walls to provide an early kind of air conditioning. The High Victorian–style interior features ceiling stenciling, ornamental plasterwork, faux-grained woodwork, heavily carved mantelpieces and stained-glass windows from the family's visit to the Columbian Exposition in Chicago in 1893.

After Neely's death in 1901, the twenty-five-room house passed eventually to his daughter, Daisy. Miss Daisy continued to live there until her death in 1969 at age ninety-eight. She made remarkably few changes to the house—keeping even the gas lights in the drawing room and music room—making it a unique time capsule of Victorian life. Miss Daisy's heirs gave the house and its entire contents to the Daughters, Sons and Children of the American Revolution to be preserved as a museum; it is now owned by the City of Memphis Division of Park Services and is open for tours.

THE TENNESSEE CLUB

130 North Court Avenue

The distinctive Tennessee Club was built in 1890, designed by architect Edward Terrell in an unusual combination of Victorian Romanesque and Moorish styles. The club was chartered in 1870 by a group of men, many of them former Confederate officers, eager to restore social graces to the city after years of Union occupation. Though organized as a men's club, the Tennessee Club established a library and art gallery and fostered

Tennessee Club, 1900. *Courtesy of Memphis and Shelby County Room, Memphis Public Library and Information Center.*

civic and scientific debates; the building's fourth floor featured a spacious domed ballroom, the scene of many elite gatherings as well as the annual presentation of debutantes.

The Tennessee Club was visited by many of the most prominent people of the time, including presidents Theodore Roosevelt and William H. Taft, senators and business tycoons. In 1908, temperance activist Carrie Nation gave a spirited speech condemning the evils of alcohol from the balcony; her speech incited hundreds of supporters to march to Beale Street and smash saloon windows. The club was also the center of business and political activity in Memphis; political boss E.H. Crump is said to have conducted much of the city's business from a luxurious meeting room known now as the Crump Room.

MAIN STREET TROLLEY

Mule-drawn trolleys ran up and down Main Street beginning in 1865. Though riding the mule cars probably beat walking the city's notoriously muddy thoroughfares, it did not come without drawbacks. Mules being mules, it was not uncommon for one to deliberately jerk a trolley car off its tracks and lie down in the middle of the street; passengers were often asked to disembark and manually lift the car back onto the tracks.

Throughout the late nineteenth century, the initial tracks expanded, and competing companies offered trolley service at a nickel a ride. Mule-drawn cars shared the tracks with the first electric trolleys starting in 1891, but it wasn't until 1895 that Memphis had a first-rate trolley system, operated by the Memphis Street Railway Company. Founded by Chicago businessmen C.B. Holmes and A.M. Billings, it ran seventy-five cars on seventeen different routes, with over one hundred miles of track. The company's lines not only connected residential areas with business and industrial areas but also ran to recreation areas beyond the city limits, fostering the growth of then suburban communities that were absorbed later into greater Memphis.

Billings died in 1897, and leadership of the company fell to his son, C.K.G. Billings. The younger Billings's true passion, however, was for fast horses; he became a leading figure on the Memphis horse racing scene, overseeing the construction of two racetracks and organizing the Memphis Gold Cup, the nation's most prestigious horse race in the days before the Kentucky Derby. When the Tennessee legislature outlawed gambling on horse racing, he sold the company in disgust to a New York syndicate and returned to Chicago.

Mule trolley. *Courtesy of Memphis and Shelby County Room, Memphis Public Library and Information Center.*

Trolley service continued until 1947 when the tracks were torn up in favor of transit buses. In 1993, the Memphis Area Transit Authority spent $33 million to bring streetcars back to Main Street with a fleet of colorful vintage trolleys on the new Main Street line. The scenic Riverfront Loop and the Madison Avenue Line were added in 1997 and 2004, respectively.

CENTER LANE

Gayoso Avenue to Barboro Alley

The buildings lining this narrow lane—the rear façades of structures fronting on Main Street and Front Street—present a unique streetscape, one of the few places in the city with largely unaltered nineteenth-century buildings on both sides of the street. It takes only a little imagination to be transported back to 1890. The metal shutters, arched windows and cast-iron columns were made locally by the Chickasaw Iron Works.

COSSITT LIBRARY

33 South Front Street

The modern building that sits on this corner is a disappointing replacement for what was once one of the city's most distinctive landmarks, a beautiful, complex Romanesque structure of red sandstone with a tall, round tower.

The Cossitt Library was the first public library in the city, built in 1893 as a memorial by the daughters of Frederick Cossitt, a Connecticut-born entrepreneur who had run a wholesale dry goods business in Memphis before the Civil War. It took the city a year to find money for books—the Cossitt family's gift was for a building only—but city newspapers called for donations of books, and the shelves soon began to fill. In the meantime, it also came to house the city's first museum collection, as people brought artifacts and curios of all kinds—everything from ancient Indian arrowheads to a taxidermied peacock—to be displayed on the empty shelves. Many of these items are on display today in the Cossitt Gallery of the Pink Palace Museum.

In the 1920s, a sympathetic white man helped a young Richard Wright use the library, which at the time did not lend to blacks. The books Wright was able to check out stoked his dreams of becoming a writer, a story recounted in his influential memoir *Black Boy*, published in 1945.

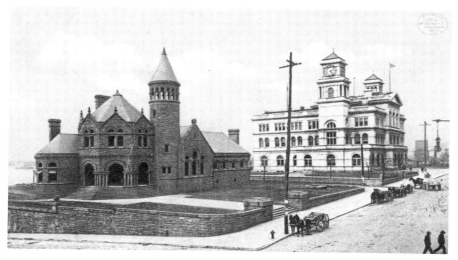

Front Street, 1908. Cossit Library and Customs House. *Courtesy of Memphis and Shelby County Room, Memphis Public Library and Information Center.*

PORTER BUILDING

10 North Main Street

Dr. D.T. Porter Building. *Courtesy of Memphis and Shelby County Room, Memphis Public Library and Information Center.*

The Dr. D.T. Porter Building, built in 1895 as the Continental National Bank Building, was the city's first skyscraper and, for many years, was the tallest building in the mid-South. When the building opened, people came from miles around and lined up to pay ten cents for an elevator ride to the roof for the view, which reportedly made many dizzy.

David Tinsley Porter—born in Robertson County, Tennessee, but raised in Kentucky—had been a pharmacist's apprentice in Nashville before moving to Memphis, where he prospered in the wholesale grocery business. He later held executive positions in banks, insurance companies, cotton firms and public utilities. After the yellow fever epidemics, he became president of the taxing district, a position akin to mayor. Porter's leadership was responsible for adopting the sewage and water system that cleaned up the city and prevented further outbreaks of yellow fever and cholera.

Porter died in 1898 and left money in his will for his family to use as a memorial. His family, however, wanted to invest in downtown real estate. A nice opportunity for compromise came when the Continental National Bank went into liquidation in 1900; the family purchased the office building and renamed it in Porter's honor. Although it is no longer the tallest building in Memphis, it remains, technically, the city's tallest monument.

ANNESDALE MANSION

1325 Lamar Avenue

This Italianate mansion was built in 1850 by Dr. Samuel Mansfield on two hundred acres on what was then the outskirts of Memphis. From 1869, it was the home of Annie Overton Brinkley—granddaughter of John Overton, one of the founders of Memphis—and her husband, Colonel Robert Snowden. The estate was a wedding gift to the couple from Annie's father, Robert Brinkley—railroad tycoon and builder of the Peabody Hotel—and was named "Annesdale" in her honor; it remained home to the Snowden family for more than 160 years. The seventeen-thousand-square-foot home has thirteen rooms, five bedrooms, four and a half baths, eleven fireplaces, a spiral staircase and a four-story tower. It is now a wedding and event venue.

Annesdale Mansion. *Author photo.*

ASHLAR HALL

1397 Central Avenue

Robert Brinkley Snowden grew up in Annesdale with his parents, Colonel Robert Snowden and Annie Overton Brinkley Snowden. In 1896, after studying architecture at Princeton University, he returned to Memphis and built this distinctive mock-castle, known as Ashlar Hall for the ashlar stone in its construction. It is said to have two underground secret passages: one underneath Lamar Avenue to Annesdale, the other below Central Avenue to the University Club.

Brinkley Snowden became one of the most prolific developers in the city, creating both the Annesdale Park and Annesdale-Snowden neighborhoods from family land surrounding Annesdale, as well as numerous other properties around the city. After Snowden's death in 1942, various restaurants occupied the house until it was purchased by Robert Hodges in the 1990s. Hodges, better known in Memphis as Prince Mongo, a self-proclaimed three-hundred-year-old alien-prince from the planet Zambodia, converted it into a nightclub called The Castle. After years of citations and noise complaints, the club was labeled a nuisance and closed.

CAPTAIN HARRIS HOUSE

2106 Young Avenue

This beautiful Queen Anne–style house, one of the oldest in the Cooper-Young Historic District, was built in 1898 by real estate developer Frank Trimble. Trimble lived in the house until Captain C.L. Harris, a railroad executive from Ripley, Mississippi, purchased it in 1900. Four generations of the Harris family lived in the home until 1935.

The house was originally surrounded by three acres of land, but in 1909, most of the land was sold to the city to be used for the Peabody School. Shortly thereafter, the house, which had originally faced east toward Cooper Street, was reoriented to face Young Avenue.

Captain Harris House. *Author photo.*

Before moving to Memphis, Captain Harris was co-owner of a railroad line in Ripley, Mississippi, along with his son-in-law R.J. Thurmond and "Colonel" William C. Falkner (as he spelled it), the great-grandfather of the writer William Faulkner. A falling out among the partners led to Thurmond shooting and killing Falkner one evening in the Ripley town square, a sensational murder that passionately divided the town. Thurmond was ultimately acquitted. Even though Harris remained an officer of the railroad alongside Falkner's son, John W.T. Falkner (the writer's grandfather) for at least ten more years, persistent local legend has it that hostile feelings against both Thurmond and Harris for the murder drove them out of Ripley to Memphis. Colonel Falkner's great-grandson William Faulkner would later use the drama in two of his novels, *Requiem for a Nun* and *The Unvanquished*.

OVERTON PARK

2080 Poplar Avenue

The city's premier park, Overton Park, was designed by landscape architect George Kessler. Named for one of the original founders of Memphis, John Overton, it opened in 1906. Typical of large urban parks of the early 1900s, Overton Park featured plantings, ponds, rustic bridges, curving drives and bridle paths and a large central greensward; in the northeast corner of the park, Kessler left standing 175 acres of virgin forest as a natural arboretum.

Noteworthy sites in Overton Park include the following.

The Memphis Zoo. The zoo traces its roots to 1906, when the mascot of the Memphis Turtles baseball team—a black bear named Natch—was tied to a tree in the park. Colonel Robert Galloway, head of the parks commission, spearheaded a drive to build a home for Natch and several other wild animals abandoned in the park in similar fashion. What began as twenty-three cages and a row of concrete bear dens has grown significantly over the years: a Carnivora House for big cats was built in 1909, followed by a Pachyderm House in 1910 and numerous other facilities, including an aquarium. The zoo is currently home to over 4,500 animals of over 500 different species and is one of only four zoos in the country to exhibit giant pandas from China. Today, most animals are seen not in cages but in ecosystem exhibits mimicking their natural habitats; the zoo consistently ranks among the best in the country.

The Brooks Museum of Art. Established in 1916, the Brooks Museum was donated to the city by the widow of Samuel Hamilton Brooks. The museum's oldest section, a Beaux-Arts building designed by New York architect James Gamble Rogers, was inspired in part by the Morgan Library in Manhattan; three large-scale additions, in 1955, 1973 and 1989, have greatly increased the exhibit areas and reoriented the entrance to the south-facing curved façade. The museum opened on May 26, 1916, without a single painting and with no permanent staff. Gifts and purchases have now brought the collection to over seven thousand works from antiquity to the present, including pieces by Pierre-Auguste Renoir, Thomas Hart Benton and Auguste Rodin along with works of African and Latin American art.

Another popular feature of the park, the Overton Park Shell, an outdoor music venue, is discussed in chapter 8. The park was the subject of a decades-long battle by grass-roots organizations and local activists against both the city and the federal government to stop construction of Interstate 40 through the middle of the park, a fight they won in the U.S. Supreme Court in 1971 in the landmark case of *Citizens to Preserve Overton Park v. Volpe*.

6

BEALE STREET

Beale Street was first laid out in 1841 as the main thoroughfare of the separate city of South Memphis, an independent river town with its own bustling landing on the Mississippi River. The two cities merged in the 1850s, and Beale Street continued to thrive alongside the older, more established Main Street.

Old-timers called Beale Street the "Stem," because it stemmed from the riverbank, and the whole city seemed to branch out from here. From the beautiful mansions on its eastern end, the whiskey dives and brothels down by the river and the stretch of small businesses in between, Beale Street was always representative of the larger city: you'd have a Chinese laundry next to a Jewish dry goods store next to an Italian grocer, across from a Greek fishmonger and a German cobbler, a truly diverse mixture in a way that Main Street never quite was.

After the disastrous yellow fever epidemic of 1878 and the loss of the city's charter, those who remained in charge of Memphis made a conscious decision to stake the city's recovery on vice: specifically, liquor, gambling and prostitution. At the time—the 1880s and '90s—two of the three were illegal in Tennessee, and the third (liquor) soon would be. But the licensing of the vice trade—the billiards halls and saloons and "dress shops" that everyone knew were fronts for brothels—led the way to the city's recovery from financial ruin, and a notorious part of Beale Street was born: Saloon Row, a hotbed of whiskey, gambling, prostitution, drugs, murder and music. On the first and fifteenth of every month, saloon owners would be charged with a misdemeanor. They would pay a cash bond to appear in court—except they wouldn't appear, forfeiting the bond to the city. It was a lucrative arrangement on all sides: for the saloonkeepers, who were largely left alone, it was a minor cost of doing business, while the city had money for its general purposes. As the *Commercial Appeal* noted in 1892, "The fire engine house on the bluff was erected from money secured from gambling houses, and the pavement in Court Square was paid for by the same process."

By the early 1900s, a wide variety of black-owned businesses lined its streets, businesses that spoke to the rising status of the city's African American population. Beale Street was the hub of it all, eclipsing for a time even Harlem as the "Negro Main Street of America." The most successful black businessmen had their offices on Beale; there were banks, hat shops, doctors, lawyers, restaurants, print shops, hotels, pool rooms, skating rinks, night clubs, anything and everything you could ever want. Grocery stores stayed open until midnight; even the fruit stands stayed open until 11:00 p.m. Street barkers selling bananas, coal, ice, ice cream, firewood, peanuts and tamales pushed carts up and down and sang out colorful songs. On Friday

Beale Street, early 1900s. P. Wee's Saloon is on the right-hand side of the street, in center. *Courtesy of Memphis and Shelby County Room, Memphis Public Library and Information Center.*

and Saturday nights, the streets were jammed from sidewalk to sidewalk with throngs of people out to have a good time. As Rufus Thomas famously said, "If you could be black for one Saturday night on Beale Street, you'd never want to be white anymore."

BEALE STREET BAPTIST CHURCH

379 Beale Street

Known as "the Mother of Black Churches," Beale Street Baptist Church is the first brick church in the South built by and for former slaves to serve their own community. The congregation originated in 1849 in praise meetings of free blacks and slaves and grew rapidly as thousands of rural freedmen flocked to Memphis during and after the Civil War. In 1865, the church raised enough money to purchase this lot on Beale Street together with lumber for a temporary shelter; the congregation worked for the next twenty-two years to pay for the magnificent church structure. It was designed by two of Memphis's leading architects of the day, Edward Culliatt Jones and Mathias Baldwin. The cornerstone was laid in 1871; the building was completed in 1885.

Beale Street Baptist Church. *Author photo.*

From 1889 to 1891, Reverend Taylor Nightengale, pastor of the church, and Ida B. Wells, a teacher at the nearby Clay Street School, published one of the earliest black newspapers in the city, the *Memphis Free Speech and Headlight*, from the basement of the church. It became the most talked-about newspaper in Memphis and gained a national circulation. In 1892, after the lynching of three African Americans who ran a grocery store in South Memphis, Wells wrote a series of articles condemning the crime and exposing the racist lies behind the practice of lynching, articles that shook the city to its core. A mob silenced the newspaper by storming the offices (then located at the corner of Beale and Hernando Streets), destroying the press and scattering the type. Luckily, Wells was away on a speaking tour at the time. Undeterred, she continued her crusade, but from a new home in Chicago: she never returned to Memphis.

CHURCH PARK

Beale and Fourth Streets

Church Park was established in 1899 by Robert R. Church Sr., one of Memphis' leading black citizens. During the Union occupation of the city during the Civil War, Church—born a slave in 1839 to a white riverboat captain and a black seamstress—embarked on a career that would establish him as a successful and respected businessman in the South. Ironically, he made a fortune by owning, operating and renting saloons and brothels. Among his first major ventures was a hotel and saloon on the corner of Second and Gayoso Streets, said to be the "finest colored establishment in Memphis." He invested heavily in real estate throughout the downtown area, especially after the devastating yellow fever epidemic of 1878, and became one of the richest men in the South.

African Americans were excluded from outdoor parks and recreational facilities in Memphis until 1899, when Church built this private park on six acres at Beale and Fourth Streets. Church's Park and Auditorium was, in its day, the grandest outdoor facility in the city, with formal walks and gardens, picnic grounds, playgrounds, a bandstand and wandering peacocks; it was said that when "lighted up at night with electricity it looks like a veritable fairy-land or garden of the gods." W.C. Handy's orchestra was a fixture in the bandstand during the summer months, and the park became a gathering spot for musicians of all types playing for tips.

Church Park. *Courtesy of Memphis and Shelby County Room, Memphis Public Library and Information Center.*

The centerpiece of the park, however, was the two-thousand-seat auditorium, which became the cultural center for the region's black community; it was the only facility of its kind owned and operated by an African American anywhere in the country. The auditorium was used for civic and church meetings, conventions, commencement ceremonies and vaudeville shows; it also functioned as a community center for political events. President Theodore Roosevelt addressed an audience at the auditorium in 1902, and the Memphis branch of the NAACP was organized there in 1917. The auditorium was the meeting place for the Lincoln League—established in 1916 by Robert R. Church Jr., son of the park's founder—to register and educate black voters.

In 1921, the auditorium was razed and a new one built in its place, which stood until the 1970s. The outline of the original foundation is marked by the columns surrounding a memorial to Robert Church Sr.

SOLVENT SAVINGS BANK AND TRUST COMPANY

386 Beale Street

Established by Robert R. Church Sr. in 1906 next door to this building, Solvent Savings Bank and Trust Company was the first African American bank in the city. It moved to this location in 1914. The bank played a crucial role in the economic development of the city's black community. By providing a sound financial base for the black community and emphasizing expansion of black-owned businesses, the bank fostered a general climate of opportunity for blacks in Memphis that was virtually unknown elsewhere in the South.

During the nationwide bank panic of 1907, when many older, established banks failed, Solvent Savings remained open; Church piled bags of money in the windows with signs stating that the bank had adequate reserves to satisfy all depositors. Solvent Savings survived the panic and became one of the leading financial institutions in the city.

MONARCH CLUB

340 Beale Street

The heart of Beale Street's old Saloon Row was between Hernando (Rufus Thomas Way) and Fourth Streets; during the thoroughfare's heyday from the 1880s to around 1910, there were fourteen saloons on the north side and thirteen on the south side. The city was controlled by a handful of underworld crime bosses: men like John Persica, who controlled the Italians on Beale and owned such places as P. Wee's Saloon; Robert Church Sr., who ran numerous saloons and bawdy houses all over the district catering to blacks; and Mike Haggerty, who would fix horse races, trials, elections or anything you liked from his headquarters at the Turf Saloon, on another street just off Beale. But the undisputed king of the crime bosses was Big Jim Kinnane, who controlled all of North Memphis and much of the rest of the city. From 1902, he held court here at the most notorious saloon on Saloon Row, the Monarch Club.

Now, ironically, a police station, in its day the Monarch was the South's finest gambling hall, featuring a beautiful mahogany bar, gleaming brass fixtures, plush velvet-cushioned seating and a mirror-walled lobby; it is also said to have had trap doors with secret exits in the case of a raid. Upstairs, a dance hall and poker rooms attracted all kinds of patrons, including W.C. Handy, who enjoyed listening to the hall's piano thumpers.

The saloon was the scene of many stabbings and shootings and murders. When someone was killed—a frequent occurrence—the bouncers would quietly take the body across the alley behind the club to a mortuary operated by the Kinnane organization. People disappeared so often this way that the club became known as the "Castle of Missing Men."

P. WEE'S SALOON

317 Beale Street

Here at this corner was once one of the most famous institutions on Beale Street, P. Wee's Saloon. P. Wee's was owned by Italian crime boss John Persica but named after Virgilio Maffei, an Italian immigrant to Memphis in the 1870s who was only four and a half feet tall. He opened his saloon in 1884 after working as a bartender at the Gallina Exchange for two years. "P. Wee" Maffei was a colorful character on the Beale Street scene; a feisty, fiery man, he once bested the famous boxer Jack Johnson in an arm wrestling match and, on another occasion, won a wager by swimming across the Mississippi from the foot of Beale Street all the way to the Arkansas side. He was quite fond of gambling, and his saloon became one of the most popular gambling dens in Memphis; high rollers from all over the country came to the saloon to play.

The saloon was a rough joint: the house slogan was "We can't close, no one's been killed yet." Like many other gambling dens in town, the saloon had elaborate warning systems to protect against police raids, including a lookout with a secret buzzer hidden in his shirt.

In the early 1900s, P. Wee's was a musicians' hangout. At the time, the saloon had the city's only pay phone, and musicians would come here to contact band leaders, especially W.C. Handy, who acted as agent for a number of different bands and selected talent from the pool of musicians at the saloon. According to legend, Handy composed his famous "Mr. Crump" (later known as "The Memphis Blues") at the saloon's cigar counter.

GALLINA BUILDING

181 Beale Street

In 1891, Judge Charles Gallina built the Gallina Exchange Building, the façade of which remains today supported by steel girders. The Gallina Exchange, once known as the Pride of Beale Street, housed a bustling saloon open twenty-four hours a day and a hotel favored by the theatrical crowd from the nearby Orpheum Theater. Judge Gallina, a Shelby County magistrate, lived with his family on the top floor and held court in a second-floor room over the saloon. The saloon was also a rowdy gambling hall popular with the horse racing set; the judge himself was a frequent denizen

Gallina Building. *Author photo.*

of the racetracks at Montgomery Park and the Memphis Driving Park and owned as many as seventeen racehorses. After Judge Gallina's death in 1914, the building was used variously as a pharmacy, clothing store, dry goods shop and dentists' offices.

The intricate brickwork and arches of the exterior hint at the magnificence of the interior. Each hotel room had a marble fireplace, and the saloon was replete with expensive walnut paneling.

The steel girders supporting the façade were put in place in 1980, originally as a temporary measure after a fire gutted the interior of the building and a subsequent windstorm caused the collapse of the rear and side walls. Plans to rebuild the structure as a hotel never materialized, and the girders are now a permanent part of the streetscape.

From the 1880s until his retirement in 1916, Edward Goens, a popular African American barber, had his barbershop in a one-story building to the right of the Gallina Building, in the space now occupied by the entrance to Silky O'Sullivan's patio. In the Jim Crow era, getting one's hair cut was maybe the least important reason to visit a barbershop; barbershops were places to meet friends, exchange news and gossip and discuss political and social events of the day. At one time, there were over fifteen barbershops within a four-block stretch of Beale.

W.C. HANDY HOUSE

352 Beale Street

This small shotgun shack was the home of W.C. Handy, the Father of the Blues, from 1912 to 1918. Originally located in South Memphis at 659 Jennette Place, this house was Handy's home when he wrote such classics as "St. Louis Blues," "Yellow Dog Blues" and "Beale Street Blues." Handy and his wife, Elizabeth, raised six children in this house. It was moved to this location on Beale Street in 1983 and is open for tours.

Handy was born in Florence, Alabama, in 1873 and came to Memphis in 1909. He became justly famous as the Father of the Blues for not only figuring out how to translate the blues into sheet music—as home-grown music invented by untrained laborers and field hands, it differed in important respects from "normal" music in the European tradition and initially baffled all who heard it—but also, more importantly, being the first to consider the music worthy of being taken seriously.

In 1909, Handy and his band moved to Memphis and established themselves on Beale Street, where there was plenty of competition. Handy began to work some of the elements of the blues into his band's arrangements. One of his most popular tunes was a song critical of young

W.C. Handy House. *Author photo.*

Memphis politician E.H. Crump, who had pledged to clean up the good times on Beale Street, something neither Handy nor any other denizen of Beale Street supported. ("If Mr. Crump don't like it, he can catch hisself some air," went the lyrics.) In the hard-fought mayoral race of 1909, Handy's band was hired by Crump to change the song to an endorsement and play it at outdoor political rallies. The band's street-corner performances drew large audiences and generated much excitement; given that Crump won the election by only seventy-nine votes, it could be argued that Handy's song made the difference in the race.

In 1912, after being rejected by several popular music publishers, the song was published under the title "The Memphis Blues." It is considered by many to be the first blues song to be published (although at least two other minor compositions titled as blues were published earlier that same year). It became an instant hit nationwide, selling over fifty thousand copies by 1913. Handy gained a huge following that established him and Memphis as important sources of the new musical style.

A. SCHWAB'S

163 Beale Street

Through more than a century and a half of change and upheaval, one Memphis business has remained unchanged: A. Schwab's Dry Goods store on Beale. Opened in 1876 just up the street from its current location, it was

A. Schwab's. *Courtesy of Memphis and Shelby County Room, Memphis Public Library and Information Center.*

still owned and operated by the Schwab family as late as 2011. It is the only original business still in operation on Beale Street and retains much of the flavor of old Beale, both inside and out.

The family business was originally located at 149 Beale and moved to its current location in 1912. In 1924, it expanded into the building to the left of the main doorway, previously occupied by the Goldsmith brothers (predecessor of Goldsmith's Department Store). Constructed in 1865, the two matched buildings feature interesting brickwork, a columned portico above the large display windows and old-style attic vents. Inside, the wood floors, glass display bins and tin ceilings recall an earlier era. The second floor features a diverse collection of items from the store's history. Although now catering mostly to tourists, the store is famous for its wide variety of unusual items, everything from left-handed scissors to size seventy-two overalls. Since its founding, the store's motto has been, "If you can't find it at Schwab's, you're better off without it."

OLD DAISY THEATER

329 Beale Street

In the 1910s, as the city's crime bosses gradually lost their grip on the city, old Saloon Row evolved into a theater district. One of the oldest and most elegant theaters was the Old Daisy, which opened in 1917 as a movie house. It was built by Sam Zerilla, a former clarinetist in John Philip

Old Daisy Theater.
Author photo.

Sousa's band. He was also responsible for the Pastime Theater, the city's first movie house for African Americans.

In 1929, the theater was the scene of the glitzy, red carpet premiere of the short film *St. Louis Blues*, starring blues legend Bessie Smith, who arrived by limousine accompanied by W.C. Handy. The Old Daisy also featured live music; despite its small stage, it was a prime performing venue on the so-called Chitlin' Circuit from the 1930s up into the 1960s.

MITCHELL'S HOTEL

209–211 Beale Street

Two all-night drugstores operated here from 1896 through the 1960s: Battier's Drug Store (until 1929) and the Pantaze Drug Store No. 2. Both operated as unofficial emergency rooms for those injured by an excess of Beale Street revelry.

Around the corner, the side door on Hernando Street (Rufus Thomas Way) was the entrance to Mitchell's Hotel, which occupied the second and third floors. The hotel was owned and operated by club owner and music

Mitchell's Hotel. *Author photo.*

promoter Andrew "Sunbeam" Mitchell, and the second-floor lounge—called the Domino Lounge and later renamed Club Handy—was one of the most popular music venues on Beale. Sunbeam Mitchell and his wife, Earnestine (who operated her own club and hotel, Earnestine & Hazel's, on South Main Street), took care of musicians, giving them meals or a place to stay when they were between gigs or low on money; it was said that Sunbeam never refused a bowl of chili to anyone with talent. Club Handy was famous for its house band—led for a time by B.B. King—and for impromptu, late-night jam sessions featuring out-of-town musicians such as Ray Charles, Little Richard, Lionel Hampton, Dizzy Gillespie and Sonny Boy Williamson.

COLORED BUSINESS EXCHANGE BUILDING

139 Beale Street

Now B.B. King's Blues Club, a series of retail businesses—a grocery, tobacco shop, liquor store, clothing store and pawn shop—occupied the ground floor of this building from the 1890s to the 1970s. The second floor contained professional offices for the black community: doctors, lawyers, dentists and insurance agents, among others. From 1944 onward, the building was known as the "Colored Business Exchange Building." Odell Horton, the first black federal judge in Memphis, had his law office here, and the second-floor offices were also the place for civil rights strategy sessions, including meetings with James Meredith, the first black student at the University of Mississippi, in the stormy days before the school was integrated.

7

PROHIBITION AND A NEW DEAL: THE CRUMP ERA, 1909–1954

Memphis in the teens and twenties was a roaring, wide-open city, a notorious drinking town where—despite Prohibition laws—alcohol was readily available in hundreds of establishments. The city was also notorious as the nation's "murder capital," with a homicide rate that was almost double the next highest city and, in some years, more than ten times the national average. (A determined campaign against vice in 1940 dramatically lowered the murder rate, and by 1960, it was the lowest of any southern city.)

Throughout it all, Memphis was dominated by Edward Hull Crump. With the help of a popular campaign song penned by W.C. Handy, E.H. Crump became mayor in 1909; he built a powerful political organization and held near-dictatorial sway over the city for the next forty-five years through Prohibition, prosperity, depression and war—leaving his mark on the city like few others. The source of Crump's power was his willingness, at the height of the Jim Crow era, to give a measure of independence to Memphis's black community. He especially encouraged blacks to vote, and while this was no doubt to some degree, maybe even mostly, a cynical tactic—there was little question who they were to vote *for*—the fact remains that Crump delivered on campaign promises and afforded the black community opportunities that were rare for the time, certainly in the South.

For a time, the city as a whole was on a rising tide. Two new train stations, Union Station (1912, now lost) and Central Station (1914), spurred the city's growth, and in 1916, Clarence Saunders sparked a retail revolution with his innovative self-service grocery store, Piggly Wiggly. The first store, on the corner of Jefferson and Main downtown, was a sensation, and in just six weeks, he opened a second. Six years later, there were over two thousand stores nationwide. Its meteoric success was due largely to Saunders's unique genius, of course, but in truth it was also timely, perfectly catching the wave of an economic boom that was sweeping across America. There was a sense of excitement and optimism in the city as Sears Roebuck opened its mammoth retail and catalogue store on the edge of town and downtown saw the construction of luxury hotels like the new Peabody Hotel (1925), ornate movie palaces like the new Orpheum Theater (1928) and high-rise office towers like the Sterick Building (1929) at Madison and B.B. King Boulevard, for years the tallest building in Memphis.

The disastrous Mississippi River flood of 1927—the most devastating flood in our nation's history, killing thousands and displacing over one million people—brought innumerable refugees to tent cities on the Memphis Fairgrounds; the city served as the headquarters and staging ground for the relief efforts run by Herbert Hoover, efforts that helped propel him into the presidency in 1928.

Cotton prices fell throughout the decade, an early sign of economic troubles to come. The stock market crash of October 1929 had little immediate effect on Memphis, but by 1931, unemployment had more than quadrupled and the Great Depression was in full swing. To help promote the cotton industry and counteract the psychological and economic effects of the Depression, city leaders created the Cotton Carnival. The first festival, in 1931, featured a parade down Cotton Row and parties and balls all over the city, drawing national attention to the city and the mainstay of its economy. (The Cotton Carnival would remain an important economic and cultural institution through the 1960s.) And under the New Deal ushered in by President Franklin Roosevelt, the city received relief programs and numerous large-scale public works projects, including several massive Tennessee Valley Authority projects in the region. Like seeds planted in a forest, many of these Depression-era projects—Lauderdale Courts and the Overton Park Shell in particular—would come into their own decades later as Memphis sprang into the spotlight in the postwar era.

CRUMP BUILDING

110 Adams Avenue

This slender building may look somewhat out of place on the edge of modern Civic Center Plaza, but for over thirty years, this office building was the center of the city's political universe. Built in 1901 as the North Memphis Savings Bank, the building became the home of the E.H. Crump Insurance Company in 1920. It was from here that E.H. "Boss" Crump controlled the city and even the state through his political machine, making this building city hall in all but name.

E.H. CRUMP HOUSE

1962 Peabody Avenue

The house was built for Edward Hull Crump in 1909, the year he was first elected mayor of Memphis. Crump was born in Holly Springs, Mississippi, in 1874. When he was just four years old, his father, a Confederate war veteran, died of yellow fever, leaving a widowed mother with three young children, of which he was the youngest. Crump dropped out of school at age fourteen to help the family make ends meet, and in 1892, at age eighteen, he came to Memphis with just twenty-five cents in his pocket. He found temporary work for a cotton broker and a real estate company but eventually was hired as a bookkeeper for a saddle, buggy and harness company.

Crump had a talent for business, a driving ambition and considerable personal charm. He rose in business and joined a number of professional and social clubs, including the Memphis Business Men's Club, of which he was elected president in 1904. In the meantime, he wooed and married twenty-four-year-old socialite Bessie Byrd McLean, the only child of Robert McLean, a prominent businessman. They were a perfect match and made an attractive couple. A newspaper account of the wedding said that Miss Bessie "has won in the few years of her young ladyhood an unsurpassed popularity by reason of her beauty and charming personality" while Crump, the article added, was "one of the most able and energetic young businessmen of the city and is possessed of a character of sterling worth that places him high in the estimate of all who know him."

Right: Crump Building.
Author photo.

Below: E.H. Crump House.
Author photo.

With his new father-in-law's help, he purchased the saddle and carriage firm where he worked and renamed it the E.H. Crump Buggy and Harness Company. But it was politics, not business, where he increasingly devoted his energies and where he was destined to make his mark. In 1905 he was named to the municipal board of public works and in 1907 won election as fire and police commissioner, a position akin to a city council seat. Two years later, as an earnest reformer and a member of the Progressive wing of the Democratic Party, he threw his hat in the ring for the mayoral race and narrowly won by a margin of only seventy-nine votes.

Crump sold his carriage business to devote himself full time to politics and in the same year moved into this house with his wife and three sons. Crump and Bessie lived here throughout his tumultuous and controversial political career, as he forged a political organization that came to control city and state politics for decades. He was elected four times as mayor, served as county trustee for eight years, and was elected to the U.S. Congress in 1930 and 1932; in 1927, he led the effort to elect Watkins Overton as mayor and handpicked every Memphis mayor after that until his death in 1954.

Crump's legacy remains controversial in Memphis. One of his accomplishments, though, was the establishment of the Memphis Park System, which may account for some of this home's beautiful landscaping: for years, the home's lawn and garden were tended by workers in the parks department.

Crump died in 1954, just three months after Elvis Presley's debut on the airwaves ushered in a new era. Bessie died two years later; they are buried together in Elmwood Cemetery.

SHELBY COUNTY COURTHOUSE

140 Adams Avenue

The Shelby County Courthouse, built between 1906 and 1909, was the first monumental work of architecture designed for local government. (Prior to this, the city and county courts were in a log cabin on the edge of Market Square and then in rented space in a hotel.) The neoclassical structure features six large, seated figures by Scottish-born sculptor John Massey Rhind, each carved from a single block of Tennessee marble. The figures represent Wisdom, Justice, Liberty, Authority, Peace and Prosperity.

7947. Shelby County Court House, Memphis, Tenn.

Shelby County Courthouse. *Courtesy of Memphis and Shelby County Room, Memphis Public Library and Information Center.*

Pediments on the Washington Street (north) façade are decorated with other allegorical figures representing Prudence, Courage, Integrity, Learning, Mercy and Temperance. It is interesting to note that over the years, two of these figures have lost their heads: Integrity (twice) and Learning. Decorations on other pediments depict the origins of law.

Until 1966, the building housed not only state and local courts but also the mayor's offices and the legislative chambers of both the City of Memphis and Shelby County.

FIRE MUSEUM AND CENTRAL POLICE STATION

118 and 130 Adams Avenue

Fire Station Number One (now the Fire Museum of Memphis) and the former Central Police Station next door were built in 1910 and 1911, respectively, and owe much of the inspiration behind their neoclassical style to the Shelby County Courthouse on the east side of Second Street. Mayor E.H. Crump, a former fire and police commissioner, was a champion of both the fire and police departments, and the buildings, constructed soon after completion of the courthouse, show his intention to elevate the status

Fire Station No. 1 and Central Police Station. *Author photo.*

of the departments and build, for the first time in the city's history, a group of monumental, inspiring public buildings.

Memphis had its first professional firefighters in 1866, but there had been a volunteer firehouse here on Adams Avenue since at least 1855; the original brick pavement can still be seen in front of the building.

The Fire Museum contains numerous exhibits on fire safety and the history of firefighting in Memphis, including uniforms, helmets and antique firefighting equipment. Several historic fire engines that were used by the Memphis Fire Department are also on display, including a horse-drawn steam engine named the "E.H. Crump" and the city's first motorized fire engine from 1912.

COTTON EXCHANGE

65 Union Avenue

The Cotton Exchange Building was the hub of Cotton Row, where the buying and selling of cotton took place.

In 1925, the Cotton Exchange returned to Front Street's Cotton Row in this building, after being located for years a few blocks away at Second

Cotton Exchange. *Author photo.*

and Madison. Following the example of New York and New Orleans, the Memphis Chamber of Commerce and other business leaders organized a cotton exchange in 1874 to bring order and information to merchants and growers. The Memphis Cotton Exchange, however, did not permit trading of cotton futures (the purchasing of cotton for delivery at a later date); instead, the Memphis exchange was a spot market, for cotton bought and sold on the spot. Today, most cotton is traded on the futures markets, but Memphis remains the nation's largest spot market for the commodity.

The old exchange trading floor is now the Cotton Museum, highlighting the story of the cotton industry and its influence on economics, history and the arts. The centerpiece of the museum is the former trading floor, restored to its appearance in the 1930s; now, as then, the trading floor is dominated by a large chalkboard showing cotton prices in different markets throughout the country.

CENTRAL STATION

545 South Main Street

Central Station was built in 1914, replacing the older Yazoo and Mississippi Valley Depot. By 1935, it was the hub of railroad transportation in the city and saw the arrival and departure of more than fifty trains a day, transporting everything from blues musicians to World War II servicemen to tourists and cargo. The station's sister depot, Union Station (now lost), was located just a few blocks east, making the South Main area the Gateway to Memphis.

Central Station is still in use today; the Amtrak train City of New Orleans, made famous by the haunting Arlo Guthrie song, stops here twice a day in its run between Chicago and New Orleans. The station has been renovated into a hotel, condos and retail space.

South Main Street and Central Station, 1943. *Courtesy of Memphis and Shelby County Room, Memphis Public Library and Information Center.*

LINCOLN AMERICAN TOWER

60 North Main Street

The Lincoln American Tower was built in 1924 as the headquarters of Columbia Mutual (later Lincoln American) Insurance Company. On a trip to New York City, Columbia Mutual's president, Lloyd T. Binford, was so impressed with the Woolworth Building—then the tallest building in the world—that he asked architect Isaac Albert Baum of St. Louis to copy it for Columbia Life. When Baum reminded Binford that the Memphis site had only one-third of the space needed, Binford ordered him to make the building a one-third replica—tower and all.

Today, Binford is most famous—or infamous—as the head of the Memphis Censor Board, a position he held from 1928 to 1955. Binford had an office on the top floor of the building, and from there, he alone decided what movies Memphians would see. Because he had once been

Lincoln American Tower. *Author photo.*

robbed while working as a mail clerk on a train, he forbade the showing of any westerns that featured train robberies. He hated Charlie Chaplin, so he refused to allow theaters here to show any Chaplin movies. When Ingrid Bergman left her husband and moved in with Italian director Roberto Rossellini, he refused to permit "the public exhibition of a motion picture starring a woman who is universally known to be living in open and notorious adultery." Classics such as *The Wild One* and *Rebel Without a Cause* were banned for promoting juvenile delinquency. Perhaps most disturbingly, he frequently cut or deleted scenes from movies that showed blacks and whites on equal social footing.

His harsh judgments of seemingly harmless films made him a household name across the nation. Publications such as *Colliers* magazine and the *New York Times* denounced Binford and ridiculed Memphis for giving him so much power. *Time* magazine quipped that "Binford has long prided himself on being able to spot a suggestive line even before it is suggested." Binford's efforts were often futile, however; theaters in Mississippi and Arkansas ran the same films, and the promotion of a movie as "Banned in Memphis" almost guaranteed large crowds from the city.

ORPHEUM THEATER

203 South Main Street

Memphis's Grand Opera House, completed in 1890, originally occupied this location. In its heyday, the Grand Opera House was known as the finest and most elegant theater outside of New York City; it housed, in addition to the theater itself, the private Chickasaw Club on its upper floors, where the elite of Memphis dined and danced. In 1907, it was purchased by the Orpheum Theater Vaudeville Circuit and featured vaudeville performances between the acts of dramatic plays. The theater burned to the ground in 1923 during a show that featured singer-comedienne-striptease artist Blossom Seeley (billed as "the hottest act in town").

In 1928, the present structure was built—nearly twice as large as the original Opera House—with gilded moldings, crystal chandeliers, lavish draperies and a magnificent Wurlitzer organ. The new Orpheum Theater featured movies and live performances from top acts such as Bob Hope, Mae West, Jack Benny, Louis Armstrong, Duke Ellington and many others. It became a Malco movie theater in 1940.

Orpheum Theater. *Author photo.*

The theater is said to be haunted by the playful ghost of Mary, a twelve-year-old girl in a white dress and pigtails, that is often seen sitting in the balcony in seat C-5. Said to have been struck by either a trolley or a carriage outside the theater and carried inside the lobby, where she died, Mary has been a fixture here since the 1920s.

PEABODY HOTEL

149 Union Avenue

After a fire in 1923 at its original location at Main and Monroe, the Peabody Hotel moved to its current location in 1925. The centerpiece of the hotel, then as now, was the magnificent lobby with its travertine marble fountain. As essayist David Cohn famously wrote in 1935:

> *The Mississippi Delta begins in the lobby of the Peabody Hotel in Memphis and ends on Catfish Row in Vicksburg. The Peabody is the Paris Ritz, the Cairo Shepherd's, the London Savoy of this section. If you stand*

Peabody Hotel, 1926. *Courtesy of Memphis and Shelby County Room, Memphis Public Library and Information Center.*

near its fountain in the middle of the lobby, where ducks waddle and turtles drowse, ultimately you will see everybody who is anybody in the Delta, and many who are on the make.

The unique tradition of the Peabody Ducks began in 1932 when General Manager Frank Schutt and his friends, relaxing in the lobby bar with some good Tennessee whiskey after a weekend hunting trip, thought it would be humorous to put their live decoy ducks in the fountain. (The use of live ducks as decoys was a common hunting practice until it was outlawed in 1935.) The ducks delighted the hotel guests, and since then ducks have been in the fountain every day. In 1940, bellman Edward Pembroke, formerly a circus animal trainer, volunteered to care for the ducks and taught them to march into the lobby, initiating the famous Peabody Duck March. Pembroke was given the title of Duckmaster and served in that position until 1991. The Peabody Duck March has become a tradition that has made the hotel famous.

The Peabody also played an important role in Memphis's musical history. During the 1920s and '30s, talent scouts for major record labels recorded local blues musicians in the hotel's guest rooms; such early field recordings, a common practice of the day, are some of the only remaining historical records of popular local performers and songs that otherwise would have been lost to memory. Later, during the 1930s and '40s, the hotel's Skyway Ballroom and its adjacent outdoor Plantation Roof featured live radio broadcast sites during the big band era. Recording engineer Sam Phillips, who managed the live broadcasts for WREC, later founded the famous Memphis Recording Service, today's Sun Studio.

PINK PALACE MUSEUM

3050 Central Avenue

The Pink Palace is a rather fanciful name given to this mansion of pink Georgia marble built by Memphis grocery store magnate and entrepreneurial innovator Clarence Saunders. A Virginian by birth, Saunders came to Memphis in 1904 as a grocery salesman; twelve years later, in 1916, he opened his first Piggly Wiggly grocery store downtown on the corner of Main Street and Jefferson Avenue. As the first modern supermarket, Piggly Wiggly not only changed the shopping experience but also revolutionized the nature of modern marketing and advertising. As to the origins of the name Piggly Wiggly itself, Saunders was intriguingly silent, though once when asked why he had chosen such an unusual name for his stores, his reply was simply, "So people will ask that very question."

By 1922, Piggly Wiggly had grown to 1,241 stores in twenty-nine states with sales of almost $200 million. Saunders began construction of this grand mansion, but in 1923, before construction was completed, Saunders went bankrupt in a stock market gambit and lost control of the Piggly Wiggly company. The unfinished house fell into the hands of his creditors and was eventually donated to the city. After spending $150,000 to complete the building, it opened as the Memphis Museum of Natural History and Industrial Arts in March 1930.

The museum was officially renamed the Pink Palace Museum in 1967. It features an exact replica of the original Jefferson Avenue Piggly Wiggly store, along with exhibits and artifacts from the mid-South's natural and cultural history, an IMAX theater and a planetarium.

The Pink Palace. *Author photo.*

LICHTERMAN NATURE CENTER

5992 Quince Road

After Clarence Saunders lost his Piggly Wiggly stores and the mansion he was building for his home, he opened a second chain of grocery stores. Irritated that the Piggly Wiggly name was "stolen" by those who forced him out, he defiantly named the new chain "Clarence Saunders Sole Owner of My Name Stores," known simply as Sole Owner stores. Saunders had a genius for entrepreneurship, and before long, there were over one thousand Sole Owner stores across the country. Back in the money again, in 1928 Saunders bought a former thoroughbred horse farm on the eastern outskirts of Memphis. In 1929, just months before the stock market crash and the onset of the Great Depression, he began construction of a seven-thousand-square foot Adirondack-style log home for his summer home; the five-hundred-acre estate included an eighteen-hole golf course, two lighted tennis courts, a lake, a boat house with observation deck, a large swimming pool, servants' quarters, an entertainment lodge, farm buildings and barns.

The estate also served as the practice field for Saunders's own professional football team, the Sole Owner Tigers, said to be one of the best independent pro teams in the country in the early days of football. In 1929, in front of boisterous crowds at Hodges Field downtown (now gone), the Tigers beat the undefeated NFL champion Green Bay Packers 20–6 and a few weeks later defeated the legendary Red Grange and the Chicago Bears by the same score; the Tigers declared themselves national champions, and few outside of Wisconsin argued. Five men on the Tigers' roster—Ken Strong, Mel Hein, Johnny "Blood" McNally, Cal Hubbard and Ernie Nevers—would later be inducted into the Pro Football Hall of Fame. In 1930, Saunders was invited to join the fledgling NFL, but he declined; he planned instead on building a sixty-thousand-seat stadium in Memphis where his team would play nothing but home games.

But deep in debt by 1932, Saunders soon lost both the team and the estate; a few years later, the estate wound up in the hands of retired baseball great Bill Terry, a Memphis native who had gone on to a Hall of Fame career with the New York Giants. Terry eliminated the golf course and many other aspects of the millionaire's playground and converted it back into a working farm and dairy.

In 1944, Terry sold the estate to a pair of brothers-in-law, Ira Lichterman and William Loewenburg, who continued Terry's cattle and dairy operations. After Lichterman's death in 1963, Loewenburg donated the estate to the Parks Commission, which ultimately led to the opening of the Lichterman Nature Center in 1977. After a fire destroyed Saunders's historic Adirondack-style mansion in 1994, a modern facility was built in 2000. Today, the Nature Center, part of the Pink Palace family of museums, is a sixty-five-acre oasis of lush gardens and wooded trails in the heart of the city, with interactive, hands-on wildlife and nature exhibits.

SEARS CROSSTOWN BUILDING

1350 Concourse Avenue

The art deco–inspired Sears Crosstown Building was the largest building in Memphis when it opened in 1927 as a Sears retail store and catalogue distribution center. The mammoth building included a soda fountain, a luncheonette, an employee cafeteria and even an in-house hospital in addition to retail and warehouse space. It was one of the largest Sears stores

Sears Crosstown Building. *Author photo.*

in the country, carrying the full line of Sears products and every item in the famous catalogue; the mail-order center featured cutting-edge technology of the day, including pneumatic tubes and a conveyor that ran throughout the entire facility.

The building was constructed during an economic boom in the late 1920s, at a time when Sears, Roebuck & Co. was expanding from rural market catalogue sales to direct retail operations in urban markets. Sears executives also recognized that automobiles made shopping mobile, and that, accordingly, retail stores no longer had to be confined to city centers, a revolutionary idea for its day. In Memphis, Sears planners met with a Memphis real estate agent in the strictest secrecy, even going so far as telling the agent to drive past prospective lots while they followed at a discrete distance in a separate car to avoid detection. They chose a large parcel of cheap land on what was then the outskirts of town but that nonetheless had good access to both rail lines and roads, perfect for both the catalogue and retail operations.

The grand opening on August 27, 1927, was a festive occasion, with speeches by Sears executives and various local luminaries, including Mayor Rowlett Paine, who also with boyish glee acted as the conductor of a special streetcar on the new Crosstown line, built especially for the store. Thousands rode the streetcar, but thousands more drove their cars and quickly filled the 1,500-space parking lot. By the end of the day, more than thirty-five thousand people—more than a quarter of the city's population—had visited the store.

Sears Crosstown weathered the Great Depression, World War II and the social upheavals of the 1960s but finally succumbed to time and progress and changing retail habits; the retail store closed in 1983, while the distribution center closed with the iconic Sears catalogue itself in 1993.

The building lay vacant for nearly twenty years until it was resurrected in a remarkable and inventive "vertical village" featuring residential, professional, retail, dining, educational and arts spaces; the new development opened on August 27, 2017, ninety years to the day of the original ribbon cutting.

MACHINE GUN KELLY HOMES

1992 Cowden Avenue and 1408 Rayner Street

One of the more infamous gangsters of the public enemy era—a time that included Bonnie and Clyde, Baby Face Nelson, John Dillinger, Pretty Boy Floyd and Al Capone—was Memphian George Barnes, better known as Machine Gun Kelly. Barnes, the son of a well-to-do insurance executive, grew up at 1992 Cowden Avenue in the upscale Central Gardens neighborhood. He attended nearby Idlewild Elementary School, then Central High School, and attended Mississippi A&M (now Mississippi State) before flunking out. Briefly married, and then divorced, he drifted from job to job and took up bootlegging, using the alias George Kelly. He was eventually caught and spent a few years in prison. It is likely he would have remained a small-time petty crook had he not met and fallen in love with a woman named Kathryn Thorne.

Kathryn—born Cleo Brooks (she thought "Kathryn" sounded more glamorous)—had been married three times before meeting George and had, if anything, more of a criminal reputation than Kelly himself. She was bound and determined to make her man famous. It was Kathryn who bought Kelly his first machine gun, a .45 caliber Thompson semiautomatic that she picked up in a pawn shop, and created the character of Machine Gun Kelly. She taught him how to use it—he is said to have "signed" his name in bullet holes on at least one occasion—and together they launched a new career of bank robbery. Kathryn, always hungry for publicity, gave exclusive interviews to reporters after a bank job and often sent souvenir shell casings to newspapermen to thank them for stories in the local papers.

The robberies gave Kelly some notoriety, but after seeing all the media attention around the kidnapping of the Lindbergh baby (in 1932), Kathryn hatched a scheme to kidnap an Oklahoma oilman and hold him for ransom. The plan succeeded: they collected the ransom and returned their victim unhurt, and the FBI designated Kelly as "Public Enemy No. 1."

The high life Kathryn envisioned was short-lived, though. The couple was soon tracked to Memphis, and in the early morning hours of September 26, 1933, Memphis police, along with FBI agents, surrounded a bungalow at 1408 Rayner Street owned by Kelly's longtime friend John Tichenor, where the Kellys were hiding out. Kelly, badly hungover from the prior evening and still in his pajamas, stepped outside onto the front porch to get the morning newspaper; when he went back inside, he forgot to lock the door behind him. The agents waited a few minutes, simply opened the door and walked in and found Kelly just stepping out of the bathroom. As legend has it, Kelly was the first to use the term *G-Man* when he raised his hands and said, "Don't shoot, G-men!"

Machine Gun Kelly boyhood home, Cowden Avenue. *Author photo.*

Kelly and Thorne were both sentenced to life in prison. Kelly began his sentence at Leavenworth, then became one of the first prisoners transferred to the brand-new federal prison at Alcatraz, where he died on his fifty-ninth birthday.

NOVEMBER 6, 1934 STREET

If you're the kind of person who gets excited about public utilities and municipal bonds, you'll be thrilled to learn that November 6, 1934 Street gets its name from Election Day in 1934, when voters approved a bond issue to allow the city to obtain electricity from the Tennessee Valley Authority. Prior to this, Memphians had electricity through a privately owned utility company, which political boss E.H. Crump had been attacking for over twenty years, calling for lower rates and public ownership. In order to plug into the TVA network, the city needed a distribution system approved by the voters; when the bond measure was finally passed by an overwhelming vote, Crump organized a celebration in Court Square and memorialized the date of his victory by renaming this narrow alley.

Although the bond issue celebrated was passed in 1934, Memphis did not receive electricity from the TVA until 1939.

SOUTHERN TENANT FARMERS UNION HEADQUARTERS

2527 Broad Avenue

The building here at 2527 Broad Avenue—now a website development office—was from 1935 to 1948 the headquarters of the Southern Tenant Farmers Union (STFU), a union of sharecroppers founded in eastern Arkansas in 1934. The STFU began in protest to the treatment of farm workers at the hands of powerful cotton barons in the South and was notable for having both integrated membership and leadership, something unheard of in any labor union of the day, let alone in the South.

When President Franklin Roosevelt took office in 1933, one of the many serious and pressing challenges he faced was an agricultural crisis, especially in the South. The general collapse of agricultural prices after World War I followed by the destructive Mississippi River flood of 1927, the 1929 stock market crash and the dustbowl drought of 1930–32, had destroyed farm income. In order to raise the price of cotton, the new Agricultural Adjustment Administration (AAA) paid planters to plow up and destroy a percentage of the crop their tenants had already planted. The federal money was meant to be shared with the sharecroppers, but many landowners kept the money for themselves and evicted their tenants, leaving them homeless and destitute. When planter Hiram Norcross of Tyronza, Arkansas, evicted twenty-three families from his plantation in late spring 1934, many of the sharecroppers—seven black and eleven white men—met in a schoolhouse with two local businessmen, and the STFU was born.

One of the local businessmen was H.L. Mitchell, a former sharecropper himself who ran a dry-cleaning business in Tyronza. Mitchell was an avowed socialist and labor activist. (Today, Mitchell's dry-cleaning shop at 117 North Main Street in Tyronza is the Southern Tenant Farmer's Museum, a fascinating museum exploring the legacy of sharecropping, tenant farming and the farm labor movement; roughly thirty minutes from Memphis, it's well worth a visit.) The STFU's main goal was to bring about a fair distribution of New Deal subsidies from plantation owners to tenant farmers and, later, to act as a collective bargaining organization, similar to the industrial unions in big cities. Many sharecroppers simply wanted to be safe from eviction and ultimately own their own land and determine their own futures. Union meetings often had the fervor of evangelical revival meetings, and as the union spread—by 1938 it had spread to six states, with thirty thousand members in over three hundred separate locals—so did violent opposition from landowners and local officials. In late 1935, after numerous shootings, beatings, fire-bombings and death threats, STFU leaders moved their headquarters to Memphis to escape intimidation. It was from this location that Mitchell and others directed union activities before moving to Washington, D.C., in 1948.

Although the union existed until 1960, it became increasingly less relevant after 1940 with the onset of World War II, the rise of mechanization of agriculture and the gradual abandonment of the sharecropping system. Though academics differ on the success of the STFU, it did result in the creation of the Farm Security Administration, which continues to aid the rural poor, as well as the LaFollette Civil Liberties Commission, which greatly aided union workers' rights generally. The STFU's legacy of blacks and whites working together also greatly influenced the early civil rights movement.

LAUDERDALE COURTS

B.B. King Boulevard between Exchange and Winchester Avenues

Lauderdale Courts—now known as Uptown Square—was a Depression-era WPA housing project, one of the first in the country. Constructed in 1938 during the days of segregation, Lauderdale Courts was a whites-only complex; another housing project, Dixie Homes (now lost), farther east on Poplar Avenue, was built simultaneously for blacks. Public housing projects today can rarely be pointed to with pride, but the Memphis Housing Authority and chief architect J. Frazer Smith created an environment that lived up to the ideals of the New Deal. The housing units were constructed around a center axis with a number of intimate courtyards that created a sense of community; from its very first days, Lauderdale Courts radiated an atmosphere of optimism. The 433 apartments featured such amenities as parquet floors and modern kitchens. With a family-income cap at $2,500 per year, the Courts gave many of its residents their first home ever with indoor plumbing.

This was true for Lauderdale Courts' most famous resident, Elvis Presley. The Presleys lived here from 1949 to 1952, while Elvis was in high

Lauderdale Courts. *Author photo.*

school. They had arrived in Memphis from Tupelo, Mississippi, a year earlier and lived in downtown boardinghouses (at 370 Washington Avenue and 572 Poplar Avenue, neither of which remains), before applying for a unit here. Lauderdale Courts was a respite for the family, a place to settle down for a while and put down some roots. For the first time in his life, Elvis had his own bedroom. Gladys, Elvis's mother, made friends with her neighbors and talked a neighbor's son, Jessie Lee Desson, into giving guitar lessons to Elvis. Jessie was nervous about this prospect, concerned that his friends—Dorsey and Johnny Burnette, musicians who were also amateur boxers—would make fun of Elvis.

Desson and the Burnettes were also friends with another musician at the courts, Johnny Black. (Johnny Black, incidentally, was the younger brother of Bill Black, who later became Elvis's bassist.) The Burnettes, Black, Desson and Elvis would often play music in the basement or the mall area of the complex.

The entrance to the Presley apartment is at 185 Winchester Avenue. The apartment itself is best seen from B.B. King Boulevard; the Presley apartment occupies the third and fourth windows on the first floor to the left of the entrance for 282 B.B. King Boulevard. Elvis's bedroom window has a small white sticker in the lower corner. The apartment has been restored to its early 1950s appearance and may be visited or rented for the night by arrangement with the Uptown Square leasing office.

8

THE MID-CENTURY MOMENT, 1954–1976

E.H. Crump died in October 1954, just as the postwar era was taking shape. But the new era—in many ways the crowning era in Memphis history to date—was ushered in by two figures inspired by the blues: a recording engineer named Sam Phillips (born in Florence, Alabama, the same hometown as W.C. Handy) and a teenager named Elvis Presley.

Phillips had come to Memphis as a radio sound engineer with a dream to record the blues, the music that Handy unleashed here nearly fifty years earlier and that still called Beale Street "home." Phillips had an ear for talent, and while he had success with Howlin' Wolf, B.B. King, Rufus Thomas and Ike Turner, it was the arrival in his studio of Presley, the "dirty kid with the sideburns," that allowed him to achieve his dream. The phenomenal, meteoric success of Elvis brought others to Phillips's door—sons of sharecroppers named Cash, Perkins and Lewis, among others—and before long, the country was moving to a new beat, a new sound created in the little studio on Union Avenue. In mid-century, Memphis had its moment on the world stage, and the world has never been the same since.

ARCADE RESTAURANT

540 South Main Street

The Arcade Restaurant is the city's oldest restaurant, having been in operation continuously since 1919. From the time of its opening to 1968,

Arcade Restaurant. *Author photo.*

the Arcade was open twenty-four hours a day, seven days a week. It is said that when it was decided to close in the evenings in the aftermath of the King assassination, no one could find the key—the door hadn't been locked in decades.

Greek immigrant Speros Zepatos founded the diner in a small, one-story, wood-framed building on this site, which was torn down and replaced with the current structure in 1925. Plans to add a hotel atop the building never materialized, but in the 1950s Speros's son, Harry Zepatos, transformed the bustling diner into the city's hippest eatery. Elvis Presley was a regular here and had a favorite booth; the interior, with its distinctive boomerang tabletop designs, has changed little since then. It is a favorite of filmmakers and photographers; scenes from *Walk the Line*, *The Firm*, *The Client*, *21 Grams* and *Great Balls of Fire*, to name just a few, have all been filmed in the restaurant.

The Arcade is still owned and operated by the Zepatos family and is a great destination for breakfast or lunch any day of the week and dinner on Thursdays, Fridays and Saturdays.

LANSKY BROTHERS CLOTHING STORE

126 Beale Street

Samuel Lansky, an immigrant from Kiev, purchased a used-clothing store on Beale Street at this location in 1946 for his sons with the idea of providing them with secure jobs as their own bosses. Under the management of Bernard Lansky and his brother, Guy, the store originally sold army surplus clothing. But Bernard Lansky, with his eyes on the colorful Beale Street nightlife parading past his store, soon changed to high-fashion custom menswear for musicians and folks stepping out on the Saturday night scene.

After a few years of business, Lansky Brothers had an impressive list of customers, including Count Basie, Lionel Hampton, Duke Ellington and B.B. King, but it was the kindness Bernard Lansky showed one day to a young Elvis Presley that cemented his reputation as Clothier to the King.

Elvis would admire the clothes in the store windows on his way to and from work at Loew's State Theater on Main Street. One day, Bernard Lansky came out to the sidewalk and invited him inside. Elvis said he didn't have any money, but said when he did, "I'm going to come back and buy you out!" Bernard replied, "Don't buy me out, just buy from me." Immediately, a friendship was formed. Elvis was used to storekeepers in Memphis and Tupelo running him off, telling him to go away because he so obviously couldn't buy anything. Bernard was the first to treat him with respect, and that meant everything to Elvis; as a result, Lansky's earned a lifelong customer.

Over the years, countless other musicians and recording artists have made a pilgrimage to the store that came to define the style of early rock 'n' roll. The list of its famous customers is a veritable who's who of music royalty: Johnny Cash, Jerry Lee Lewis, Carl Perkins, Roy Orbison, Isaac Hayes, Frank Sinatra and many more.

The store—still operated by the Lansky family—relocated to the lobby of the Peabody Hotel in 1981 but returned to this original location with a second store in 2016.

SUN STUDIO

706 Union Avenue

Sun Studio is the name given to this remarkable recording studio that literally changed the world. Aptly described as the Birthplace of Rock 'n' Roll—the first rock 'n' roll single was recorded here in 1951—the studio also launched the careers of Elvis Presley, Johnny Cash, Jerry Lee Lewis, Carl Perkins, Roy Orbison and a host of others.

Originally known as the Memphis Recording Service, the studio was opened by Sam Phillips in January 1950. Phillips came to Memphis at age twenty-two to work for radio station WREC. Phillips had bigger plans, however. He had been captivated by the blues since his youth, and in January 1950, he followed his dream of opening his own recording studio. Although the studio's motto was "We Record Anything—Anytime—Anywhere," Phillips's aim was to record the great blues musicians he heard on Beale Street; he was convinced that this music could gain mainstream acceptance if given the chance.

Phillips signed a lease on this small storefront and opened his doors to such local talent as B.B. King and Howlin' Wolf. Initially, he leased

Sun Studio. *Author photo.*

the recordings to out-of-town independent labels; among these early recordings was "Rocket 88," a single by Jackie Brenston and his Delta Cats (with Ike Turner on the piano) that, for its unintended use of guitar distortion—the band's amplification equipment was damaged and was "fixed" with newspaper wadded up and stuffed around the speaker cone—is credited as the first rock 'n' roll song.

After losing some of his most promising talent to other record labels, Phillips decided to launch his own label, Sun Records, in March 1952. For the first two years, Sun Records released a string of blues recordings, along with some hillbilly and gospel numbers. During this time, Phillips became convinced that his records would sell if he could make black music more accessible to a white audience. Then, in 1954, a nineteen-year-old kid named Elvis Presley started hanging around the studio. At first, Phillips was unimpressed by Elvis's attempts at crooning popular hits, but when he broke out one night into "That's All Right," a song first recorded by bluesman Arthur "Big Boy" Crudup, Phillips found what he had been looking for. Elvis brought a hillbilly sound to the music while retaining the spirit and energy of black rhythm and blues, and rockabilly was born.

Elvis recorded ten singles at Memphis Recording Service for Sun Records and became an international star. The studio's direction changed dramatically. The phenomenal success of Elvis brought other white musicians to Phillips's door: artists such as Johnny Cash, Jerry Lee Lewis and Carl Perkins all launched their careers at Sun Records. On the strength of hits such as Cash's "Folsom Prison Blues," Perkins's "Blue Suede Shoes"—the first million-seller for Sun Records—and Lewis's instant classics "Whole Lotta Shakin' Going On" and "Great Balls of Fire," Phillips outgrew the tiny studio and moved to larger digs around the corner at 639 Madison Avenue in 1959.

The studio lay vacant until 1987, when it was reopened as Sun Studio, a working studio and tourist attraction. It was designated as a National Historic Landmark in 2003. The twenty-by-thirty-five-foot studio is considered hallowed ground by many of the world's leading entertainers; bands and performers such as U2, Ringo Starr and Tom Petty have all recorded here, hoping to catch a bit of the magic within its walls. The excellent one-hour studio tour is highly recommended for anyone with an interest in Memphis music.

The building on the corner adjacent to the white storefront studio was once Taylor's Restaurant; it is now the Sun Studio gift shop. Sam Phillips had a regular booth in the café and would often do paperwork or meet with musicians here over a cup of coffee and a bite to eat. The checkered floor and tin ceiling are original to the restaurant. Upstairs was a boardinghouse; Jerry Lee Lewis, Carl Perkins, Roy Orbison and many others rented rooms here while working at the studio next door.

HOTEL CHISCA

262 South Main Street

When the Hotel Chisca opened in 1913, it was the largest and grandest hotel in the South Main district. The Chisca contained Turkish baths, a barbershop, a liquor store, a beauty parlor, the Yellow Cab Company, a cigar store and a green room lounge for performers from the nearby Orpheum Theater.

The Chisca is most famous as the home of radio station WHBQ and the groundbreaking *Red, Hot & Blue* program hosted by Dewey Phillips. Broadcasting from the hotel's "magazine floor"—the mezzanine—Dewey

Hotel Chisca, 1934. *Courtesy of Memphis and Shelby County Room, Memphis Public Library and Information Center.*

Phillips was one of the pioneering deejays who, along with Cleveland's Alan Freed, is credited with promoting the new sound of rock 'n' roll. Dewey started his radio career in 1949 and was the city's leading radio personality for close to ten years.

Phillips's on-air persona was a speed-crazed hillbilly with a frantic delivery and entertaining sense of humor. He also had a keen ear for music the listening public would enjoy, and he embraced both black and white music. Along with programming on rival station WDIA, Phillips's influential show *Red, Hot & Blue* did much to bridge the artificial racial barriers of the 1950s.

In July 1954, Phillips was the first deejay to broadcast Elvis Presley's debut record, "That's All Right," playing it numerous times in a row and causing a sensation among the city's teens. Elvis's first radio interview was also conducted at the Chisca by Phillips.

OVERTON PARK SHELL

1928 Poplar Avenue

The Overton Park Shell, built in 1936, was one of more than two dozen amphitheaters constructed by the WPA during the Depression; it is one of the few remaining today.

The Memphis Symphony Orchestra performed in the shell's opening night concert before a crowd of six thousand, but the shell's most famous

Overton Park Shell, 1930s.
Courtesy of Memphis and Shelby County Room, Memphis Public Library and Information Center.

concert was Elvis Presley's performance here on Friday, July 30, 1954. The show—advertised as a Hillbilly Hoedown featuring yodeling cowboy Slim Whitman—was Elvis's first paid concert appearance. Though his first record, "That's All Right," was a hit on local radio stations, he was still so unfamiliar that advertisements and concert posters billed him as "Ellis Presley." When he stood up on the balls of his feet and shook his leg in time with the music—something he often did in the studio—the girls in the audience went crazy. Offstage, after his frantic, two-song set, Elvis asked the concert promoter, Bob Neal, "What'd I do? What'd I do?" Neal is said to have replied, "I don't know, but go back out there and do it again."

GRACELAND

3764 Elvis Presley Boulevard

Without a doubt the best known Memphis landmark and its most-visited attraction, Graceland—the residence of Elvis Presley—was once part of a five-hundred-acre farm owned by Stephen C. Toof, a Memphis printer and publisher. The name "Graceland" is an old one, first given to a nineteenth-century house here in honor of Toof's daughter, Grace. The house was replaced in 1939 by the present house, but the name continued.

Elvis purchased the home in March 1957 for $100,000 when he was just twenty-two years old. His parents, Vernon and Gladys, discovered it while on a Sunday drive and, noticing the "For Sale" sign, brought it to his attention; for some time, Elvis had been looking for a place to live with more privacy than their East Memphis ranch house. On 13.8 acres, surrounded by farms and pastures, it seemed perfect.

The house quickly became a destination for fans, and the stone wall and famous gates were installed for privacy in April 1957. Over the years, Elvis added other buildings, structures and landscape features to the property, including a racquetball court and the Meditation Garden, where his mother—and later Vernon and himself—was buried. The interior—decorated largely by Elvis's wife, Priscilla—remains pretty much as it was at Elvis's death in 1977, including the famous Jungle Room with its outsized Polynesian-style furniture.

Fans clamored at the gates for autographs or a glimpse of the King, and once two teenage girls sealed themselves in a box and tried to get on the grounds disguised as a package delivery. Still, Graceland was a refuge for

Graceland. *Courtesy of Elvis Presley Enterprises.*

Elvis, a sanctuary where he could relax and be himself, horse around with his buddies and spend time with those he loved.

Elvis died here of a heart attack in August 1977; his viewing and funeral was one of the largest ever in Memphis, with over 3,500 mourners filing through the foyer, with many more fans mourning outside.

The house has been open to the public since 1982 and is one of the most visited homes in the country. A tour of the mansion includes the greatly expanded visitor center, containing a car museum, two of his custom jet airplanes and various special exhibits as well as the Entertainer Career Museum, a twenty-thousand-square-foot museum celebrating Elvis's extraordinary life and career.

STAX MUSEUM OF AMERICAN SOUL MUSIC

926 McLemore Avenue

Stax Records—renowned for soul music—was founded, ironically, by two white businesspeople, Jim Stewart and his sister Estelle Axton. Stewart was a banker and bond salesman, working at the First National Bank downtown while moonlighting as a fiddle player with several local country bands. Like many other Memphians in the wake of the phenomenal success of Elvis Presley and Sun Records, he dreamed of making it in the music business. In 1958, he convinced his sister Estelle to take out a second mortgage on her house for $2,500 to pay for recording equipment and set up a small studio in a rented store in Brunswick, just outside of Memphis. The location—in proximity to railroad tracks—proved less than desirable, and in 1960, they moved their operation here to the former

Capitol movie theater on McLemore Avenue, renting the space for $100 a month. In the old theater, they combined a record shop, run by Axton, and a recording studio. The sloping theater floor with carpeted walls and heavy bass movie theater speakers would create the distinctive sound of Stax recordings.

Stax produced such major artists as Otis Redding, Isaac Hayes, Rufus Thomas, Carla Thomas, Wilson Pickett, William Bell, Johnnie Taylor and Sam & Dave. In 1971, Hayes won an Academy Award for Best Song for the theme from the movie *Shaft*; he was the first African American to win an Oscar in a music category.

Stax's fortunes began to change with the loss of Otis Redding, the most beloved Stax artist, in a plane crash in December 1967. Redding's final hit, "(Sittin' on the) Dock of the Bay" was released posthumously and became one of the studio's most successful recordings. Stax was still reeling from Redding's death when Atlantic Records merged into Warner Brothers and canceled its distribution agreement with Stax. At the same time, Stax learned that it was Atlantic, not Stax, who held ownership of all the prior Stax masters, as well as the recording contract with Sam & Dave.

The studio regrouped and continued to release hits into the early 1970s, but in 1976, after years of financial scandals, it closed its doors for good. The vacant building was torn down in 1989.

Over a decade later, the Stax Museum of American Soul Music was constructed at the site and opened in 2003. A replica of the original building, the Stax Museum features exhibits on the history of Stax and soul music in general, and hosts various music-related community programs and events; on display are Isaac Hayes's 1972 gold-plated Cadillac El Dorado, an authentic one-hundred-year-old Mississippi Delta church, and clothing and personal items from a wide range of stars. An afternoon at the museum is highly recommended.

Stax Museum of American Soul Music.
Courtesy of the Stax Museum of American Soul Music.

The adjacent Stax Music Academy is a state-of-the-art facility mentoring youth of the Soulsville neighborhood through music education and unique performance opportunities; the building also houses the Soulsville Charter School.

HI RECORDS/ROYAL STUDIO

1320 Willie Mitchell Boulevard

Royal Studio is the home of Hi Records, founded in 1957. The studio had some initial success recording the Bill Black Combo (Elvis's former bass player), Ace Cannon, Willie Mitchell and others in the mid-1960s before moving into the soul genre for which it is most famous today, with such artists as Al Green and Ann Peebles.

Royal Studio is still an active recording studio. Bruno Mars and Mark Ronson's hit "Uptown Funk" was recorded here in 2014 and, in 2016, won a Grammy award for Record of the Year; in 2019, the song was named Billboard's top song of the decade.

Like Stax Records just a short distance away on McLemore Avenue, Royal Studio is housed in a former movie theater. The conversion and repurposing of small movie houses was common in the late 1950s and early 1960s with the newfound popularity of television.

ST. JUDE'S-ALSAC PAVILION

262 Danny Thomas Place

The world-renowned St. Jude Children's Research Hospital is one of the most significant developments in Memphis in the latter half of the twentieth century. The hospital is a leading pediatric treatment and research facility focused on children's catastrophic diseases. In 1996, Dr. Peter C. Doherty received a Nobel Prize for medicine for his work here, and St. Jude's remains at the forefront of advances in cancer treatment.

The hospital was founded in 1962 by actor and comedian Danny Thomas. In 1941, Thomas, then a struggling young entertainer, knelt in a church before a statue of St. Jude—patron saint of hopeless causes—and asked the saint to "show me my way in life, and I will build you a shrine." Not long afterward, he received an unexpected break in show business, and soon his career flourished. By the early 1950s, he was an internationally beloved (and well-paid) entertainer. Not forgetting his vow, Thomas and a group of Memphis businessmen developed the idea of building here a unique hospital and research center.

The son of Lebanese immigrants, Thomas (whose real name was Amos Alphonsus Muzyad Yakhoob) turned to other Americans of Arab-speaking

St. Jude Children's Research Hospital and Danny Thomas   *Photo by Don Lancaster*

Danny Thomas and St. Jude Children's Research Hospital. *Courtesy of Memphis and Shelby County Room, Memphis Public Library and Information Center.*

heritage to help with fundraising and founded the American Lebanese Syrian Associated Charities (ALSAC) in 1957. Today, ALSAC is the exclusive fundraising organization for St. Jude's. In front of the hospital, the gold-domed ALSAC Pavilion resembles a Mediterranean-style mosque and features exhibits and memorabilia of Danny Thomas's career in entertainment and the history of St. Jude's. Thomas, who died in 1991, and his wife, Rose Marie, are buried in a crypt in the Pavilion's garden.

MID-SOUTH COLISEUM

996 Early Maxwell Boulevard

For more than forty years, from 1963 to 2006, the Mid-South Coliseum was the premier sports and concert venue in the area; it was the site of legendary concerts by both Elvis and the Beatles as well as the Stax-Volt Revue, Ike and Tina Turner, The Who, Led Zeppelin, the Rolling Stones, James Brown and just about every other significant performer of the era. It was also the scene of sporting events such as Memphis State's (now University of Memphis) thrilling run for the national basketball championship in 1973, ice hockey games and professional wrestling, including the infamous, iconic match between Jerry "The King" Lawler and comedian Andy Kaufman in 1983.

Developed and constructed between 1960 and 1964, it was the first public auditorium in Memphis to be planned as an integrated, race-neutral facility, an extraordinary thing for its time and place. (A similar municipal arena in Mobile, Alabama, for example, opened two years later with segregated entrances and restrooms.)

The live concert album, *Elvis Recorded Live on Stage in Memphis*, came from a series of shows Elvis performed here in 1974; it resulted in one of only three Grammy awards Elvis would win during his lifetime, for Best Inspirational Performance, "How Great Thou Art."

Even more legendary than the King's series of sold-out shows were the matinee and evening concerts of the Beatles on August 19, 1966. It was the group's second (and last) American tour, with Memphis the only southern city on the tour. The tour as a whole, and especially the Memphis show, was plagued with backlash from John Lennon's controversial remarks in an interview that the Beatles were "more popular than Jesus." Despite numerous explanations and Lennon's televised apology, the Memphis mayor and city council called for the cancellation of the concert rather than have "municipal facilities be used as a forum to ridicule anyone's religion." Conservative groups staged public burnings of Beatles records,

Mid-South Coliseum. *Author photo*.

and a group of ministers planned a Memphis Christian Youth Rally at Ellis Auditorium downtown on the same night "to give the youth of the Mid-South an opportunity to show that Jesus Christ is more popular than the Beatles."

The day of the concert was "a very tense and pressured kind of day," according to the band's press agent. The Beatles received a number of death threats and rode past angry protestors lining the streets on the way to the Coliseum. Outside the arena, Ku Klux Klan members in full regalia marched and handed out anti-Beatles literature, a sight that unnerved the band.

Despite the protests, the shows went on. The Beatles played two shows, at 4:30 p.m. and 8:00 p.m. The first show went smoothly, with typical adoring—and screaming—fans. Between shows, the four patiently answered questions from the media about the "bigger than Jesus" controversy and talked about their interest in recording in Memphis. They admired the stars of Stax Records and wanted to work with Steve Cropper, the guitarist and producer. ("He's the best we've heard," they said.) The second show got off to a good start and seemed to be going well until a fan, presumably as a prank, threw a firecracker on stage. The *bang* terrified the Beatles, Lennon especially, and though the band kept on playing, everyone was looking at one another, certain one of them had been shot.

The Beatles finished out the 1966 tour and never toured again, though George Harrison brought his own band to the Coliseum in 1974.

OVERTON SQUARE

Madison Avenue and Cooper Street

In 1969, a twenty-three-year-old named Jim Robertson—described in a newspaper article as "youthful, brash, articulate, iconoclastic. Somewhere out there between The Graduate and Easy Rider"—bought a former insurance office on Madison Avenue near Cooper Street and converted it into a coffeehouse and hangout called Perception. He soon had bigger plans, though, after visiting a jam-packed bar in New York City called T.G.I. Friday's, one of the first "singles bars" in the country. Back in Memphis, he gathered together a group of friends and acquaintances, the oldest of which had just turned thirty, and leased additional business property along Madison Avenue with an eye toward opening a Friday's franchise, the first outside of New York City.

They faced one significant obstacle: in 1969, it was against the law in Memphis for a restaurant to serve liquor by the drink. (To have a drink or a glass of wine with dinner, you had to bring your own bottle.) Richardson and his partners led the effort to overturn the law, and when a special referendum measure passed on November 25, 1969, they formed a corporation called Overton Square Inc., the very next day, and announced their intention to transform Memphis nightlife.

Friday's opened in May 1970 and was quickly a smashing success; it paved the way and became an anchor for shops, restaurants, pubs and other attractions on Madison Avenue. The Overton Square shopping and entertainment district was ahead of its time in many respects—in 1970, downtown Memphis was still suffering from suburban flight and the aftereffects of the assassination of Martin Luther King Jr., while Beale Street had become primarily pawn shops, most of which would close over the course of the decade. The main shopping centers of East Memphis were dull in comparison to the Square, and except for Ellis Auditorium downtown, there were no decent venues for touring musicians. All of that changed with the opening of Lafayette's Music Room and a dramatic expansion of the Square to include more shops, more restaurants, even an ice skating rink. A newspaper article at the time called it "Memphis' version of Greenwich Village, Bourbon Street, and Gatlinburg all rolled into one." Acts like Linda Ronstadt, Barry Manilow and Billy Joel routinely played at Lafayette's; Joel later credited the exposure from his Lafayette's shows (including one broadcast live on radio) as helping launch him from a minor opening act to a genuine star. Pub crawls and street fairs attracted over forty thousand people at a time, and Christmas at Overton Square was known for its carolers, roasted chestnuts and snow from snow machines mounted on the roofs of buildings.

The Square's popularity eventually faded as other venues and entertainment districts were developed, and Friday's itself closed in 2003. The Square was brought back to life in 2012, though, and is once again one of the premier entertainment districts in the city.

9

CIVIL RIGHTS AND
THE AFRICAN AMERICAN EXPERIENCE

African Americans were some of the earliest residents of Shelby County. The 1820 census, recorded a little more than a year after the city's founding, listed 55 black males and 67 black females out of a total population of 374. All were slaves.

Memphis always had a complicated relationship with slavery. Tennessee had a strong antislavery movement at the time when Memphis and Shelby County were settled, and the city grew to have a small but significant population of free blacks. Up until the 1830s, free black men had most of the same legal rights as white men, including the right to vote. Most free blacks were manual laborers, craftsmen or domestic workers, but some owned property and businesses, including Joseph Clouston, who at one point owned downtown real property worth in excess of $20,000, quite a large sum for that day. In the decades just before the Civil War, however, the legal status of free blacks deteriorated, and by the 1850s, free blacks had to register with the county court and pay a bond to remain in the community.

Following the Civil War, the lot of African Americans improved considerably. Blacks enjoyed some political gains and saw the growth of African American churches and benevolent societies. Blacks were instrumental in keeping the city alive during the yellow fever epidemics of the 1870s. In 1878, in the midst of the worst outbreak, African Americans numbered close to 70 percent of the population that remained in the city and they provided virtually the entire workforce for the community. They collected and buried the corpses, distributed the relief supplies that poured in from the nation and served as nurses for the sick and dying. Two companies of black militia patrolled the streets to protect property and prevent looting. In the 1880s, under the taxing district, blacks served together with whites on the police force, on the school board and in lesser offices of the city administration. African American leader Robert Church Sr., a sharp but prudent self-made millionaire who had been born a slave, displayed faith and optimism in the city's future by purchasing some of the early bonds to fund repayment of the city's debt and restore its charter. Others both black and white followed his example, and the city slowly clawed its way out of darkness. The city's charter was restored in 1893.

It was, nonetheless, still a segregated city, in many ways rooted in cruelty, and while the city grew and prospered, the gains were not enjoyed by all. Reversing ingrained habits and attitudes proved to be difficult, and as the nation moved deeper into the turbulent twentieth century, tensions remained. The pace of change was too slow for many blacks; for many whites, who saw the traditional social structure crumbling around them, it was just the opposite. A strike of city sanitation workers brought the tensions boiling to the surface. The point of no return was reached on April 4, 1968, when Dr. Martin Luther King Jr. was assassinated on the balcony of the Lorraine Motel, one of the darkest days in Memphis's—and indeed the nation's—history.

BURKLE ESTATE/SLAVEHAVEN

826 North Second Street

Jacob Burkle, a German immigrant, came to Memphis in the mid-nineteenth century and opened a stockyard and bakery on the north end of town. He built this simple white frame house in 1849, known today as the Burkle Estate, in a then sparsely populated area north of the Gayoso

Burkle Estate. *Author photo.*

Bayou. A trap door and hidden chambers under the house support local lore suggesting that the house was once a waystation on the Underground Railroad for runaway slaves prior to the Civil War. Now a museum, the house features exhibits and artifacts from slavery days and the slave trade in Memphis.

ZION CHRISTIAN CEMETERY

1426 South Parkway East

Zion Christian Cemetery is the oldest African American cemetery in Memphis, established in 1873 by the United Sons of Zion, a black fraternal and benevolent organization, under the leadership of Reverend Morris Henderson, the founding pastor of Beale Street Baptist Church. Active until 1925, it has more than thirty thousand graves in its fifteen acres. During the yellow fever epidemic of 1878, many Memphians fled the city, but the cemetery's Pallbearers Association remained to help prevent looting and maintain order in the city; many of them succumbed to the fever and are buried here with other black victims. It is also the burial place of Thomas

Zion Christian Cemetery. *Author photo.*

Protests in Memphis continued throughout the summer of 1960, coordinated with a campaign of boycotts, demonstrations and lawsuits filed by the local NAACP. The suits and protests were ultimately successful and resulted in the full integration later that year of downtown lunch counters, movie theaters and restaurants as well as the public library, city buses, the Pink Palace Museum, the Brooks Museum, Overton Park and the Memphis Zoo.

MASON TEMPLE

938 Mason Street

Built in 1940, Mason Temple is the world headquarters of the Church of God in Christ, a historically African American Pentecostal denomination. Designed with Art Moderne details, the temple seats close to four thousand people on two levels. It was named for Bishop Charles Harrison Mason, founder of the Church of God in Christ, who is entombed in a marble crypt inside.

Mason Temple was one of the focal points of civil rights activities in Memphis during the 1950s and 1960s and was the site of Martin Luther King Jr.'s prophetic "Mountaintop" speech on April 3, 1968, the evening before his assassination. The speech primarily concerned matters relating to the Memphis Sanitation Strike. Toward the end of the speech, however, King referred to threats against his life and used language that seemed to foreshadow his impending death:

> *We've got some difficult days ahead. But it doesn't matter with me now. Because I've been to the mountaintop. And I don't mind. Like anybody, I would like to live a long life. Longevity has its place. But I'm not concerned about that now. I just want to do God's will. And He's allowed me to go up to the mountain. And I've looked over, and I've seen the Promised Land. I may not get there with you. But I want you to know tonight, that we, as a people, will get to the Promised Land.*

SANITATION STRIKE OF 1968

The 1968 Sanitation Workers' Strike, culminating in the assassination of Dr. Martin Luther King Jr., shook Memphis and the nation to the core. For sixty-five days, as winter slowly gave way to spring, Memphis was gripped in a bitter struggle, a struggle not just about better working conditions or higher wages, but about fundamental notions of justice and human dignity. "I Am a Man," the placards said, a simple, powerful message that still resonates today. The strike began and ended in tragedy. Quite a number of locations around the city are still extant.

Colonial Road near Sea Isle Road

On February 1, 1968, two black sanitation workers, Echol Cole and Robert Walker, both in their thirties, took cover during a sudden rain squall by ducking inside the back of a sanitation truck. The truck malfunctioned, and the two were crushed to death. The accident happened near this intersection in East Memphis, but it could have happened anywhere. In fact, two other men had died under almost the exact same circumstances four years earlier, but the Department of Public Works—under then-commissioner Henry Loeb, who was now mayor—had refused to update or modernize the department's equipment.

Though city flags flew at half-mast for Cole and Walker, their families received only a token death benefit, not even enough to pay for the funerals.

United Rubber Workers (URW) Local 186
1036 Firestone Avenue

On Monday, February 12, the sanitation workers held their first official strike meeting. At a rousing meeting the previous evening held to discuss the frustrations and grievances that had been building for some time, the workers had roared approval of a strike when it became clear that the director of public works would not address their concerns. On the following morning, so many workers showed up at their regular union hall on Second Street (since demolished) that the meeting was moved to a larger hall: the United Rubber Workers Local 186 hall near the Firestone Factory. Daily mass meetings would occur here at noon each day throughout the strike, with afternoon marches to city hall—a three-mile walk.

Colonial and Sea Isle Roads. *Author photo*.

Union Hall, United Rubber Workers. *Author photo*.

City Hall and Civic Center Plaza,
Main Street between Poplar and Adam

City hall held the offices of Mayor Henry Loeb and the city council chambers. Dozens of marches and demonstrations occurred here throughout the strike. On February 23, police using mace attacked strikers on nearby Main Street. On March 5, more than one hundred strikers and their supporters staged a sit-in inside city hall after a compromise proposal was rejected by Mayor Loeb. On March 8, after several union leaders were jailed, strikers staged a mock funeral in Civic Center Plaza for the "death" of freedom in Memphis.

Centenary United Methodist Church
584 East McLemore Avenue

The largest black Methodist church in Memphis, it was led by Reverend James Lawson. Lawson served as chairman of the strike committee and was a major figure in the civil rights movement. Dr. Martin Luther King Jr. called Lawson "the leading theorist and strategist of nonviolence in the world." It was at Lawson's request that Dr. King came to Memphis to dramatize the workers' struggle against the city.

Clayborn Temple
280 Hernando Street

Clayborn Temple was an important center of the black community throughout the civil rights years and was the rallying point for the sanitation workers during the strike. The strikers gathered daily here at the Temple and marched to city hall.

By mid-February, the daily marches were regularly met with force by the police. After one particularly bloody day in February, the Reverend James Lawson gave a rousing address to the strikers here and said, "At the heart of racism is the idea that a man is not a man, that a person is not a person. You are human beings. You are men. You deserve dignity." In the audience that day was Reverend Malcolm Blackburn, who, in addition to being Clayborn's minister, was also a printer and sign maker and had a full printing press in the church basement. He created the iconic "I Am A Man" placards for the strikers and printed them here.

City hall, 1967. *Courtesy of Memphis and Shelby County Room, Memphis Public Library and Information Center.*

On March 28, Dr. King came to Memphis and led fifteen thousand people from Clayborn Temple to city hall in what was supposed to be a nonviolent demonstration, but the march ended abruptly with violence breaking out on Beale Street. It proved to be a major turning point of the strike, a watershed day setting into motion a chain of events that would culminate in Dr. King's assassination at the Lorraine Motel less than a week later.

The march was scheduled to start at 10:00 a.m. from Clayborn Temple, proceed north on Hernando Street (today that part of the route would pass through the FedEx Forum), turn west on Beale Street, then north on Main Street to city hall. It was a beautiful day, bright and sunny, with temperatures in the mid-sixties. After a late start, Dr. King began the march, linking arms with Lawson and other local leaders; estimates of the size of the crowd behind them varied from six to twenty thousand. As Dr. King and the head of the column turned onto Main Street from Beale, they heard behind them the ominous sound of breaking glass. Marchers in the back, fueled by the frustration of the previous months, used sticks, pipes and bricks to smash storefront windows on Beale. The Memphis police, ready for trouble, moved in with mace, tear gas and nightsticks.

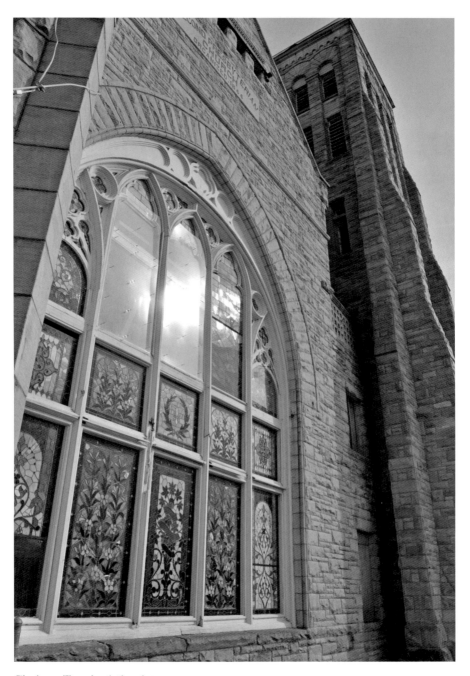

Clayborn Temple. *Author photo.*

Fearing for Dr. King's safety, Lawson ordered King's bodyguards to remove him from the scene immediately. Meanwhile, the police attacked the crowd on Beale and pursued marchers back to Clayborn Temple. Demonstrators fought with the police outside while others sought refuge inside. Police fired tear gas through the doors of the Temple; for years afterward, the marks from the canisters could still be seen on its walls. Hundreds were arrested, over sixty injured and one person killed in the rioting that went on across the city through the night.

Holiday Inn Rivermont
655 Riverside Drive

Now luxurious high-rise condos known as the River Tower at South Bluffs, this was the location of the Holiday Inn Rivermont, where Dr. King was taken after rioting ensued on Beale Street during the March 28 march. Dr. King—against his will—was whisked into a car at Front Street and Peabody Place (then called McCall Avenue) to the hotel. In the weeks that followed, stories in the *Commercial Appeal* and elsewhere blasted King, the "prophet of the poor," for "fleeing" to the luxurious Rivermont while chaos broke out in the city. To counter this, King insisted on staying at the Lorraine Motel on his return, despite increasing concerns for his safety.

Lorraine Motel
406 Mulberry Street

The Lorraine Motel, owned by Walter Bailey and his wife, Lorene, was the premier African American hotel and motel in Memphis. When Dr. King and his right-hand man, Ralph Abernathy, checked in here in April, they were given their usual room, 306, the largest in the motel. Abernathy remarked that they had stayed in that room so often during their visits to Memphis that it was jokingly referred to as the "King/Abernathy Suite."

On the evening of April 4, King planned to attend a dinner at the home of a local minister. In an upbeat mood, dressed for dinner and waiting for Abernathy to join him, he walked out onto the balcony, joked with some of his staff and spoke briefly to associates in the parking lot below. Seeing horn player and bandleader Ben Branch, who was to perform at a rally later that night, King called down to him, "Play 'Precious Lord' tonight, will you?

Lorraine Motel. *Author photo.*

Play it real pretty." Moments later, at 6:01 p.m., a single shot rang out ("like a stick of dynamite," in the words of a witness) and King fell. Rushed by ambulance to St. Joseph's Hospital (where St. Jude's Children's Research Hospital now sits), King was pronounced dead within the hour.

Lorraine owner Walter Bailey suffered not only the loss of his friend Dr. King but also a more personal loss that evening. His wife, Lorene, working the hotel's switchboard at the time, had a cerebral hemorrhage upon hearing the news of King's assassination. She never recovered from the shock and died five days later on April 9.

The Lorraine Motel, and indeed the entire neighborhood, declined steeply in the aftermath of the assassination. Bailey was forced to declare bankruptcy in 1982, and the motel was ordered to be sold on the courthouse steps. On the morning of the auction, a group of Memphis businessmen purchased it with plans to remodel it as a lasting shrine to Dr. King and the movement he led and inspired. Their plans evolved into today's National Civil Rights Museum, which tells a powerful story of the civil rights movement from slavery to the present day.

Fire Station No. 2
474 South Main Street

The area around the Lorraine swarmed with FBI agents and Memphis city police in the days leading up to the assassination. Law enforcement agents kept watch on Dr. King from a small hole in newspaper plastered across the windows of the fire station overlooking the Lorraine. Their role was not to protect King, but to see who he met with and watch for signs of an impending riot.

Young & Morrow Building
422 South Main Street

In 1968, this building housed the Canipes Amusements Company. A restaurant called Jim's Grill occupied the building next door. Between the two buildings was a narrow doorway (now marked 418), which led to a rooming house in the upper floors operated by Bessie Brewer. It was from a window in the second-floor bathroom at the rear of the rooming

Young & Morrow Building. *Author photo.*

house that James Earl Ray fired on King. Ray, an Illinois native and longtime criminal, had, according to the FBI, been tracking King since mid-March.

Ray dropped a duffel bag in the doorway of Canipes Amusements as he fled the scene; it contained a Remington rifle with Ray's fingerprints, a scope and a pair of binoculars purchased by Ray just hours before the killing. In the confusion following the shooting, Ray managed to escape the city. A massive manhunt ensued before Ray was ultimately apprehended by British authorities in London while attempting to board a flight to Brussels.

R.S. Lewis & Sons Funeral Home
374 Vance Avenue

On Friday, April 5, the primary wake for Dr. King was held in the home's chapel, which filled with thousands of mourners wishing to view the body. King's casket was then flown to Atlanta for two more funeral services.

10

COLLIERVILLE AND GERMANTOWN

Collierville and Germantown were both founded in 1836, and both prospered in the decades before the Civil War as stops on the Memphis and Charleston Railroad. Collierville was named for its founder, land speculator Jessie Collier, but no one is quite sure how Germantown got its name. While there were a few families of German descent in the area, the residents were overwhelmingly Irish or Scots-Irish. In fact, the community was known as Pea Ridge until 1836, when a surveyor named N.T. German was hired to lay out the town lots and streets. His name is on the original plat as surveyor, but he lived in Holly Springs, Mississippi, and had little or no other connection with the town; there is little reason to think that that he would be honored for his work by having the town named after him. Be that as it may, the town was incorporated as Germantown in 1836.

Both towns strongly supported the Confederate cause in the Civil War. On April 15, 1861, the same day that President Lincoln called for seventy-five thousand volunteers for the Union, eighty young men of Collierville—over 15 percent of the town's population—organized a unit for the Confederacy called the Wigfall Grays. Tennessee at the time was still in the Union, though it would officially secede just a few months later in June; the Wigfall Grays subsequently became Company C of the Confederate army's Fourth Tennessee Infantry and fought in some of the bloodiest battles of the war, including Shiloh, Murfreesboro, Chickamauga, Missionary Ridge, Atlanta, Franklin and Nashville.

The war first came home to Collierville with the arrival of a train full of wounded soldiers from the Battle of Shiloh. Many of the wounded were carried to the Methodist church, where the ladies of Collierville sprang into action with bandages, bedsheets and blankets, some even bringing table linens from their homes to make into dressings. Collierville was occupied by the Union army a few months later in June 1862 and would remain in Union hands for the remainder of the war.

Collierville has the unique distinction of being the site of not one, but two of the war's great *what if?* moments. In June 1862, General Ulysses Grant came through the area on his way to Memphis and stopped at the house of one Josiah Deloach on the outskirts of Collierville. Alerted by a neighbor, Rebel cavalry rode hard through the midday heat to capture him, arriving only forty-five minutes after he had left. Given the heat, the state of their horses and Grant's head start, they decided it was fruitless to pursue him any further, unaware that Grant and his staff had stopped again in a grove of shade trees less than a mile from the house. Had the Confederates ridden just a few minutes more, they very likely would have captured General Grant.

A little over a year later, on October 11, 1863, Major General William Sherman was almost killed in a Collierville battle that proved to be the biggest battle in Shelby County. Traveling by special train from Memphis to Chattanooga, he happened to roll through Collierville just as 3,000 Confederates descended on the town. Sherman ordered the train to back up into the depot and deployed what men he had to bolster the 250 soldiers that made up the town's Union garrison. Moments before the telegraph wires were cut, he sent a message up the line to Germantown and Memphis to hurry reinforcements.

A small but fierce battle ensued, and as the three thousand Confederates attacked the depot, Sherman calmly walked among his men and directed the defense. At one point, as bullets whistled all around him, a sergeant begged Sherman to take cover; Sherman told him to mind his own business. In his memoirs, Sherman wrote that "the enemy closed down on us several times, and got possession of the rear of our train, from which they succeeded in getting five of our horses, among them my favorite mare, Dolly; but our men were cool and practiced shots (with great experience acquired at Vicksburg), and drove them back." The Confederates kept up the attack for three to four hours until Union reinforcements arrived.

Collierville saw another, smaller battle later in the year and numerous skirmishes and small actions in the vicinity. By the end of the war, the town had nearly disappeared—only three buildings remained standing.

It lost its corporate charter and officially ceased to exist. Collierville was reincorporated in 1870 on ninety acres somewhat to the west of the original town, and it was this second incarnation of Collierville that gave life to what remains its most charming feature, the historic town square.

Germantown saw similar destruction; it was burned on July 23, 1862, and was occupied for the remainder of the war. Reverend Richard Evans, minister of the Presbyterian Church, persuaded a Union officer to spare the church because they were both Masons; the church and the Masonic lodge were used as a hospital and stable and were the only buildings left untouched. By war's end, the town's population had been reduced by half. Churches and homes were slowly rebuilt, but like its big-city neighbor Memphis, Germantown suffered an outbreak of yellow fever in 1878; nearly half of all persons infected died in just a few days.

The late 1940s saw the birth of the Germantown Charity Horse Show. Originally a gathering of horse-owning friends interested in fox hunting and trail rides, the event has grown to be one of the oldest and largest in the nation.

COLLIERVILLE HISTORIC TOWN SQUARE

Town Square Park was laid out in 1866 and became the centerpiece of the reincorporated town in 1870. Originally named Confederate Park, it was enclosed with a white picket fence and contained roaming peacocks and a tame deer. A two-story lattice-work bandstand was constructed in the center of the park in 1876, but it was destroyed by a tornado in 1955; the current bandstand dates to 1994. Many of the buildings around the square

Collierville Town Square and Stagecoach Stop. *Author photo.*

date from the late 1800s and today house a mix of boutiques, specialty shops and museums. The square remains the heart of historic Collierville and is still used for festivals and special events.

COLLIERVILLE DEPOT

Rowlett Street

The current railroad depot building is actually the third in this general location. The original depot—the one that played such an important role in the 1863 Battle of Collierville—was built in 1852 and is believed to have been a block west, on the north side of the tracks between Center and Walnut Streets. It did not survive the war. In 1885, a new depot was built slightly east of the original, with a large cotton platform on one side and an icehouse on the other. In 1944, the Southern Railway Company tore it down and, because building materials were scarce during World War II, replaced it with the depot from LaGrange. The building was cut in half and transported—by train, of course—to a new location just to the east of the old one. In 1976, the railroad donated it to the city, where it now serves as the town's tourism center.

Nearby are a number of items from the town's railroad history: a 1912 steam engine of the Frisco Railroad; a Southern Railroad caboose; and an executive rail car, the Savannah. The engine, no. 1351, is a 2-8-2 steam engine weighing 230 tons and was operated for over forty years on the Frisco Railroad. It was retired in 1952. The Savannah railcar, designed for the comfort and convenience of the railroad executives as they traveled the lines, is little changed since it was built for the Seaboard Railway in 1915; it includes two suites, a dining room, a kitchen, an observation room, a valet's room and crew's quarters.

COLLIERVILLE STAGECOACH STOP

Town Square

Built in 1851, this log cabin was used as the Collierville area's stagecoach stop for many years in the mid- to late 1800s. Once located a short distance west at Byhalia Road and South Rowlett Street, it was moved to the town square in 1977 and rebuilt with the original logs.

MORTON MUSEUM OF COLLIERVILLE HISTORY

196 Main Street

The Morton Museum is an excellent local history museum, housed in a former church built in 1871. The museum tells the entire story of Collierville, from the earliest Native American inhabitants of the area to the establishment of the town, the coming of the railroad, the Civil War and after and has numerous special programs, workshops and regularly scheduled events for adults and children alike. Admission is free.

JOHN GRAY HOUSE

Germantown Municipal Park

The John Gray House is the oldest brick home in Shelby County, built before 1851. Gray, a native of Kentucky, moved to Shelby County in the 1840s and established a prosperous cotton plantation in the Morning Sun community

John Gray House. *Author photo.*

some nine miles northeast of Germantown. The small, two-room house with an attic loft is a Georgian hall-and-parlor design that, while common in tidewater Virginia, was rare in West Tennessee.

In 1989, the house was saved from destruction and moved to the present site along with historic and prehistoric artifacts from the original site.

FORT GERMANTOWN

3085 Honey Tree Drive

On January 13, 1863, Union major general James B. MacPherson deployed a number of small detachments to secure the Memphis and Charleston Railroad and protect it from Rebel attack. He ordered that "at all the points to be guarded, defensive stockades must be constructed to render the command safe against a sudden cavalry dash." "Fort Germantown" is a rather grand name for one such stockade, a modest earthen fortification built by the Union army in early 1863 at a strategic curve in the rail line. The outpost, properly known as a redoubt, was manned by a small detachment

Fort Germantown. *Author photo.*

from an Illinois regiment. Over a dozen raids and small actions were fought in the area, though the small redoubt itself was never attacked.

In the autumn of 1863, Union troops in the area were sent east to the siege of Chattanooga. The soldiers burned the wooden palisade on top of the earthen walls before abandoning the site; it was never reoccupied.

Two replica cannons guard the fortification today. While the redoubt was of only minor importance during the war, it is quite valuable today as one of the few surviving examples of a small unit outpost widely used during the war and has yielded much archaeological information on both earthwork construction and daily garrison life away from the front lines.

GERMANTOWN PRESBYTERIAN CHURCH

2363 South Germantown Road

This plain but beautiful church was built in 1851, though the congregation dates back to 1838. Out of the town's population of 250, more than 50 men—almost every able-bodied man in the town, and many of them

Germantown Presbyterian Church. *Author photo.*

members of this congregation—had joined the Confederate army, but when in 1862 the Yankees came to burn the town, the minister, Reverend Richard R. Evans, convinced the Union officer to spare the church because they were both Masons. The church, having survived the ravages of war and yellow fever, is today Germantown's oldest surviving public building.

The distinctive bell tower was added just after the Civil War, in 1867; in the 1950s, the church was reoriented from facing north to east and was eventually converted into the chapel of a new, larger sanctuary added to the south.

GERMANTOWN TRAIN DEPOT

2260 West Street

The Germantown Depot, originally dating to shortly after the Civil War, was reconstructed after a fire in 1948, using many of the original timbers. It was a working train station until 1986 and now houses a train museum, with two waiting rooms—a relic from the days of segregation—and a baggage room big enough to accommodate bales of cotton.

Germantown Depot. *Author photo.*

OAKLAWN GARDEN

7831 Poplar Pike

If Germantown had an attic, it would be Oaklawn Garden. Swiss immigrant Fritz Hussy acquired the 1875 farmhouse and twenty acres of land in 1918. He was joined by his daughter, Mamie Cloyes, and her husband, Harry (whom she later divorced), and together they operated the property as a commercial flower farm and nursery called Oaklawn Gardens. Mamie continued running the business after Fritz's death, and in 1968 turned the business over to her son, Harry, and his wife, Becky. By the 1960s, Oaklawn had over 2,000 azaleas, along with 6,000 bedding plants, native dogwoods, redbuds, flowering shrubs, ornamental trees and 350 varieties of daffodils. Many of these remain on the property today. In the meantime, Harry had begun collecting historic artifacts, and the grounds also became something of an informal local history museum.

On the property are old railroad cars and crossing signals, old city signs, electrical transformers, water fountains, fire hydrants, traffic lights, a 1942 fire truck and Germantown's first jail—a narrow bunk bed surrounded by a heavy, no-nonsense iron grating. The quaintness of Harry's collection makes a stroll through the grounds fascinating and fun. Following the death of Harry in 2011, then Becky in 2015, Oaklawn became part of the Germantown park system and is free to the public.

11

BARTLETT

In 1847, young Gabriel Maston Bartlett moved to Shelby County from Cedar Hill in Middle Tennessee. Newly married, he bought over 450 acres next door to his cousin John Blackwell in what was then known as Greenbottom. He became active in local affairs and was elected a justice of the peace and, later, a state representative. Historical accounts note that he was tall with dark auburn hair and blue eyes and had both a fine singing voice and an impressive "presence," and became known as "Major Bartlett." After the death of his first wife, he remarried in 1853 and bought additional property in the area, over 300 acres just west of the railroad depot where the Memphis and Ohio Railroad crossed Stage Road.

Bartlett's home, a "handsomely finished frame six room house, a new cotton gin and corn mill, slave quarters, apple, plum, and peach orchards," was on the north side of Stage Road between what is now Sycamore View Road and Old Brownsville Road. In 1858, he had the surrounding land surveyed for a town and donated lots for a school, a church and a Masonic lodge. The town—variously known as Greenbottom, Union Station or Union Depot—prospered; it was incorporated in 1866 and named Bartlett in honor of Gabriel, who served as the first mayor.

Major Bartlett, though a slaveholder, was a Northern sympathizer during the Civil War, but it didn't prevent his farm and orchards from being nearly destroyed by the war. In 1864, in an attempt to revive his financial fortunes, he went into business with two partners as grocers, cotton factors and commission merchants on Front Street in downtown Memphis. After struggling through the final years of the war and its aftermath, the business went into bankruptcy in 1868.

Bartlett sold off much of his land, including his house and the remaining town lots, to his cousin Dr. Nicholas Blackwell and his business partner, Dr. William Pryor. In 1875, Shelby County decided to build a courthouse in Bartlett due to its more central location in the county, and Blackwell and Pryor donated a lot on the corner of Court and Woodlawn Streets, just a few blocks from the county's exact geographical center. A two-story building was used as the courthouse until 1885. Today, Bartlett High School sits on land, also donated to the town by the Blackwell family, adjoining the old courthouse property.

Cotton was the major agricultural product for much of Shelby County from the very earliest days, and there were three gins in the Bartlett area. But in the 1920s, due to both the boll weevil and the plummeting of cotton prices after World War I, Bartlett turned to dairies to diversify the local economy. The town had two full-blown processing plants on Stage Road and Raleigh-LaGrange Roads, with many smaller operations in the surrounding area; by the 1930s, there were over twenty dairies in Bartlett.

Bartlett lost many fine historical structures in a great fire that spread through the town in 1923. Several remain, however, and are worth a look.

DAVIES MANOR

9336 Davies Plantation Road

Davies Manor is the oldest existing house in West Tennessee. It is said to date to the 1820s, with additions in the 1830s. From 1851, it was the home of two brothers, James Davies and Logan Davies, sons of Reverend William Davies, a Methodist minister in Fayette County.

The earliest recorded owner of the property is Thomas Henderson, who in 1821 was granted 640 acres for his service in the American Revolution. By 1830, he had sold half of his land to an Emmanuel Young, who, just a year later, lost the property by defaulting on his taxes. It was purchased by the tax collector, Joel Royster, who made significant additions to the house, expanding it from one room to two stories by 1837. In 1851, Logan and James Davies bought the house and additional acreage from Royster and named it Davies Plantation; it remained in the Davies family until 1994.

Dr. William Davies in front of Davies Manor, 1875. *Courtesy of Davies Manor Association.*

In 1854, James married Penelope Little of Collierville and had two sons, Julius and William, who grew up to be doctors. Penelope died in 1859 at age twenty-eight. The following year, 1860, on the eve of the Civil War, Logan married Frances Vaughn, and the two families shared the log house. Davies Plantation at this time consisted of 792 acres and twenty-two slaves.

At the outbreak of the war, James enlisted in the Confederate Thirty-Eighth Tennessee Infantry and fought in numerous engagements, including Perryville, the Second Battle of Atlanta, Lookout Mountain, New Hope Church, Nashville, Peach Tree Creek and Jonesboro.

On the homefront, Logan and Frances and their slaves maintained the house and plantation throughout the war. They cared for James's young sons and had two children of their own, a son, Gillie, in 1861 and a daughter, Lillie Lee, in 1863. The war and the raiding and foraging of two armies across the land had lasting effects on those both at home and on the battlefront. The house was visited repeatedly by soldiers from both sides during the war; on one occasion, according to family tradition, Frances Davies, with a kitchen knife hidden in the folds of her skirts, confronted a Union officer who tried to take her horse and other livestock during a foraging expedition. When the officer refused to give her horse back, she is said to have grabbed the bridle and cut the reins with her knife. "Sir," she told the officer, "I have my horse. You go." And he went.

James returned home from the war in May 1865, a changed man. He married Pauline Little, his late wife's sister, and attempted to return to his former life, but he was deeply disturbed by his military experiences, by all accounts suffering from what would now be recognized as posttraumatic stress disorder; Pauline later obtained a divorce—a rare occurrence at that time.

The legacy of slavery also had long-lasting effects. Slave life continued at Davies Plantation during the war despite the Union occupation of West Tennessee; as late as 1865, Logan Davies was earning income by renting out enslaved people to neighboring plantations. James Davies took along an enslaved "bodyservant" named Richmond Bennett with him when he joined the Confederate army. After the war, Richmond returned with James to Davies Plantation and, as a free man, married Sarah Tucker, another former Davies family slave. Richmond, Sarah and their children lived in eastern Shelby County well into the twentieth century. At least half a dozen other people formerly enslaved by the Davieses worked as sharecroppers at Davies Plantation throughout the nineteenth and early twentieth centuries.

In 1976, Ellen Davies Rodgers, the daughter of Gillie Davies and the last descendant of either Logan or James, donated the house to the Davies Manor Association for tours. The house, along with numerous outbuildings, including a tenant cabin, a plantation commissary, a gristmill and an outhouse, are open to the public and are well worth a visit. The property also contains several gardens, including a kitchen garden and a medicinal herb garden.

GOTTEN HOUSE

2969 Court Street

Nicholas Gotten was a German immigrant who came to the area in the 1850s. During the Civil War, he rode with General Nathan Bedford Forrest's cavalry and served in the Battles of Shiloh and Corinth. He was badly wounded in 1863, taken prisoner and later exchanged and returned to Forrest's Third Tennessee Cavalry through the end of the war. After the war, he became a respected miller and cotton ginner, and when the town of Union Depot incorporated as Bartlett in 1867, he was elected the first

Gotten House. *Author photo.*

constable. A few years later, he built this New England–style saltbox home on Court Street.

Gotten and his wife, Julia, raised three children in the house, and it remained in the family until 1948, when it was purchased by the City of Bartlett for use as a police station and jail. The Gotten House is currently the home of the Bartlett Historical Society Museum, open on the first and third Sundays of each month.

BLACKWELL HOUSE

3077 Sycamore View Road

In 1865, Dr. Nicholas Blackwell moved to Union Depot to begin a medical practice and manage the estate of his uncle John Blackwell, who had owned hundreds of acres in the area. Nicholas, who had served as a captain in a Mississippi company of the Confederate army during the Civil War, became one of the town's more influential leaders and was instrumental in incorporating the town in 1866. He was elected one of the first aldermen and served several terms as mayor.

Blackwell House. *Author photo.*

After acquiring most of the unsold town lots from Gabriel Bartlett after Bartlett's financial difficulties, Blackwell and his partner Dr. William Pryor made generous donations of property for civic purposes, including the lot for the courthouse and later, a school (the current home of Bartlett High School). As a country doctor, he was a beloved figure in the town, often seen making house calls on horseback at all hours of the day and night; it's been estimated that at the turn of the twentieth century, Dr. Blackburn had been on hand for the delivery of nearly half of Bartlett's population.

In 1866, Nicholas married Lucy Ward, daughter of another prominent family in the area, and two years later they had a daughter, Willie. The following year, he began construction on a two-story Gothic Revival home on the corner of Sycamore View Road and Blackwell Street, featuring a beautiful circular staircase, wide, dark polished pine plank floors and floor-length windows. The Blackwells moved in during January 1871, but tragically, Virginia died only a few days later. Blackwell never remarried but raised his daughter in the home with the assistance of his niece. He practiced medicine and lived in the house until his death in 1910; Louise, one of his daughter Willie's children, lived in the Blackwell house her entire life, until her death in 1982 at age eighty-eight.

12

ARLINGTON

Arlington is a charming town, and one of the oldest communities in Shelby County; at the time of the Chickasaw Cession, there were already close to twenty families living in the area. The community, prospering on cotton, grew to around two hundred people by 1856, when the Memphis and Ohio Railroad came. A depot was constructed on land donated by local landowner Samuel Jackson Hays, a nephew of President Andrew Jackson, and the town acquired the name of Haysville in his honor.

Like every other community in West Tennessee, the town suffered from the raiding and foraging of armies both North and South during the Civil War. Samuel Hays, who had attended West Point, was offered a position as a Confederate general by his old friend Jefferson Davis. Hays declined, but he outfitted a company for the Confederate service.

A series of yellow fever epidemics in the area in the 1870s put a further damper on growth, especially in 1878, when the town fathers quarantined the area, forbidding outsiders from entering the town in hopes of keeping the fever out.

Nonetheless, Haysville had about five hundred inhabitants when it was incorporated in 1878. In 1883, when the town leaders wanted to establish a post office, they discovered there already was a Haysville, Tennessee; the name was changed to Arlington on the suggestion of a town resident who had recently visited Arlington National Cemetery in the nation's capital and thought it was the most beautiful spot on earth.

By 1900, the town was reincorporated officially as Arlington and boasted two cotton gins, five general stores, a sawmill, several livery stables, a physician, a druggist, a meat market and a blacksmith. Today, Arlington is one of the fastest-growing communities in Tennessee, but its small-town charm remains. Historic Depot Square has a number of historic structures as well as a replica of the old train depot, and throughout the town, many houses and old landmarks have been preserved.

S.Y. WILSON STORE

12020 Walker Street

Samuel Young Wilson was born in 1865 in the neighboring town of Hickory Withe to a former private in the Confederate army and his young bride from Mississippi. Samuel was the oldest of the couple's eighteen children. After an apprenticeship as a bookkeeper to a store in Arlington, he took a course at a business college in Memphis and returned to open his own general store in 1893.

Originally a wooden frame building, the present two-story brick building was built in 1913. Over the years, Wilson's sold everything from groceries to hardware, farm implements, dry goods, feed and seed and gifts and antiques. There is no comparable modern counterpart to a store like Wilson's; its place in the community was always more than strictly commercial, where men swapped news and gossip, talked business and politics and spat tobacco around the pot-bellied stove. Local farmers used their crops as collateral for supplies, and Wilson in effect acted as banker to his customers, extending credit and holding a lien on their crops. Come harvest time, farmers sold their crop then settled up at the store to repay the lien, and seldom had much, if any, money left over. With its inherent inequalities, it was a system ripe for abuse and injustice, and many in Wilson's position all over the South were known to take advantage. Though there were some in Arlington who naturally harbored a degree of bitterness toward the man and his family who controlled so much of the town's economic life, S.Y. Wilson was nonetheless remembered fondly at his death in 1955 as a kind man who "carried people over" and helped with financial problems.

The S.Y. Wilson store also housed the town's first fire truck, purchased in 1949. Prior to this, fires were handled by community bucket brigade: to report a fire, one would telephone the switchboard at the town's central telephone exchange, which was operated by a brother-and-sister team, Richard and Johnnie Pope. The telephone office was located on the second

S.Y. Wilson Store. *Author photo.*

floor of a store on Depot Square; Richard would lean out of the window, fire a pistol three times, wait a few seconds, then fire again. As people ran to the square at the signal, Richard and his sister Johnnie would yell from the windows what direction to take.

DEPOT SQUARE

6271 Chester Street

In addition to a replica of the original depot, now a senior center, Depot Square displays the HARRELL FARM LOG CABIN, a plantation cook's house built in the mid-1800s and relocated here. It's open for tours to see a rope bed and other artifacts of country life. Next to it, the restored historic POST OFFICE, built in 1885, displays interesting items of postal history as well as artifacts honoring the town's veterans. On the west side of the square is a BLACKSMITH SHOP, a recreation of the original shop that stood here from the late 1800s to 1991. The forge, restored in 2003, is one of the few working forges in Tennessee, and blacksmithing demonstrations are given throughout the year during special events.

RACHEL H.K. BURROW MUSEUM

12020 Walker Street

This was built in 1905 as a bank—Arlington Bank & Trust—for many years the town's only financial institution. When the bank failed in the Great Depression, the building was used as a community center and, later, a doctor's office. In 1957, when the doctor moved his office, it housed the town's first library, and for close to twenty years, the mayor and aldermen used it as town hall. When a new and modern town hall was built in 1980, it became finally a museum of local history, named in honor of Rachel Herring Kennon Burrow, the town historian. It currently displays local historic items and changing special exhibits.

Rachel H.K. Burrow Museum. *Author photo.*

13

NORTH SHELBY COUNTY

Much of North Shelby County has changed little since the earliest days, with orchards and fields and small rural hamlets. Today, the region is dominated by Millington, for many years home to a Naval Air Station. But remnants of the past remain in the rural communities, several of which date from the early 1800s; they are some of the oldest settlements in West Tennessee and are worth taking an afternoon to explore.

BARRETVILLE

Barret Road

Anthony R. Barret, born in Kentucky but raised in Tipton County, Tennessee, settled in the area that was to become known as Barretville with his wife, Rebecca, in 1852. He started a general store that grew into a large and prosperous business. After Anthony's death in 1910, his son James Hill Barret continued the business under the name of J.H. Barret & Son. When it closed its doors in the 1990s after more than 130 years, it was the oldest continuously operating business in Shelby County.

The Barret family store grew into a commercial empire that eventually included four additional general stores in the surrounding area as well as six cotton gins, a cottonseed delinter plant and thousands of acres of farmland. In 1920, at the age of twenty-one, Paul W. Barret, grandson of Anthony

J.H. Barret & Son General Store, Barretville. *Author photo.*

Barret, founded Barretville Bank & Trust Company, which eventually grew into one of Tennessee's largest rural banks, with branches and allied banks in towns all across the region. Paul Barret was also deeply involved with Shelby County politics; he was an ally of E.H. "Boss" Crump and served as circuit court clerk and then a member of the county quarterly court for over twenty years, earning him the title of squire, as members of the quarterly court are traditionally known.

In 1975, at the age of seventy-five, Barret happened to be on the floor of the Barretville Bank when a lone bank robber entered wearing a ski mask and holding a pistol. Paul kept his cool and said to the robber, "Son, this is just a country bank, we don't have any money here." The robber believed him and fled empty-handed.

Neither Paul Barret nor his quick wit were present on the night of May 10, 1931, when thieves used blow torches to try to cut through the wall of the vault from the adjoining general store; the attempt was unsuccessful—no money was taken—but both buildings burned to the ground. The bank and the store were rebuilt—in separate, freestanding buildings—and still stand today.

Paul Barret's home, Squire's Rest, built in the 1920s across the street from his parent's home, is in the National Register of Historic Places. Domesticated Indian peacocks, descendants of the original peafowl raised by Paul's wife, Sarah, can often be seen alongside or even crossing Barret Road off State Route 14.

Barrettville is also the birthplace of blues musician Bobby "Blue" Bland. Born Robert Calvin Brooks, he later took the name of his stepfather. Bland grew up singing for fifty cents a song at the Barret cotton gin as the cotton wagons waited their turn. Noted for his synthesis of blues and gospel, he was known as the "Sinatra of the blues"; his most memorable songs include "Further On Up the Road," "Turn On Your Love Light" and "(They Call it) Stormy Monday." In 1992, he was inducted into the Rock and Roll Hall of Fame, which described him as "second in stature only to B.B. King as a product of Memphis's Beale Street blues scene"; he is also an inductee in the Blues Hall of Fame and Memphis Music Hall of Fame.

ROSEMARK

Rosemark Road and Kerrville-Rosemark Road

Rosemark is a residential and farm community in northeastern Shelby County that was listed in 2006 in the National Register of Historic Places. In the late 1800s and early 1900s, farms and farm communities like Rosemark made up more than 70 percent of Shelby County; the cotton economy defined much of the area for generations.

Originally known as Richland, Rosemark was first settled in the 1830s. For most of its history, it was an agricultural crossroads community with a cotton gin and community facilities. The community's first school, Richland School, opened in 1861. Much of the community's growth, including the formation of churches and the establishment of stores and the cotton gin, occurred during the decades following the Civil War. When applying for a post office in 1890, the town learned there already was a "Richland" in East Tennessee, so everyone gathered in the general store and put names in a hat: Rosemark was drawn and became the new name of the town. By the turn of the twentieth century, Rosemark had at least three general stores, a cotton gin, a bank, a blacksmith, a beauty shop and other small businesses. In 1912, the community got its own telephone company, which, together with the Richland—now Rosemark—School, extended the community's influence over a wide area.

The Moore family came to Rosemark in 1886 from Lincoln County, Tennessee, and quickly established themselves as one of the preeminent families in the community. In 1896, they opened a general store, no longer in use but still standing on the southwest corner of the intersections of Rosemark

Rosemark cotton gin. *Author photo.*

and Kerrville-Rosemark Roads. Across the road, they also operated a cotton gin, a lint house and a cotton warehouse; all three buildings still stand, though no longer in use. The Moore family farm, Harmoore, was located at 8703 Rosemark Road and was the center of the family's farming operations; the old farm office building still exists where sharecroppers and tenant farmers settled accounts with the Moore family; a tenant house still exists as well, the last of three tenant homes built on the property.

SHELBY FOREST GENERAL STORE

7729 Benjestown Road, Millington, Tennessee

No excursion into the north county would be complete without a stop at the Shelby Forest General Store, an old-time country store that has changed little either in appearance or character since the 1930s.

Original owners Emmet and Dixie Jeter opened the store in the summer of 1934 as a general dry goods store offering "a little bit of everything." In 2003, after being operated for decades by the Jeter and McFarland families and close family friends, it was nearly razed and replaced with a gas station;

Shelby Forest General Store. *Author photo.*

it was rescued by Doug and Kristin Ammons, who lovingly maintain it in all of its authentic charm.

The Jeters added a grill to the store in the 1940s, and the General Store evolved into a community gathering place for neighborhood residents, including, in recent years, actor and musician Justin Timberlake, who grew up in the area and went to nearby Jeter Elementary School. (Timberlake even mentioned the store on stage in the 2009 Grammy awards.) The grill features southern delicacies like fresh-made biscuits, fried bologna sandwiches and catfish fillets—and a popular steak night every Friday—while the store carries groceries, snacks, beer, live bait and basic supplies. Friends and old-time residents still gather on the front porch and exchange the most current gossip.

Situated near the two entrances of Meeman-Shelby Forest State Park, the store is a popular stop for tourists and visitors as well as locals and is well worth a visit.

SELECTED BIBLIOGRAPHY

Biles, Roger. *Memphis in the Great Depression*. Knoxville: University of Tennessee Press, 1986.

Bond, Beverly, and Janann Sherman. *Memphis in Black and White*. Charleston, SC: Arcadia Publishing, 2003.

Capers, Gerald M., Jr. *The Biography of a River Town: Memphis, Its Heroic Age*. New Orleans, LA: Tulane University Press, 1966.

Coppock, Helen M., and Charles W. Crawford, eds. Paul R. *Coppock's Mid-South*. Four vols. Memphis, TN: Paul R. Coppock Publication Trust, 1985–94.

Coppock, Paul R. *Memphis Memories*. Memphis, TN: Memphis State University Press, 1980.

———. *Memphis Sketches*. Memphis, TN: Friends of Memphis and Shelby County Libraries, 1976.

Dowdy, Wayne G. *A Brief History of Memphis*. Charleston, SC: The History Press, 2011.

———. *Mayor Crump Don't Like It: Machine Politics in Memphis*. Jackson: University of Mississippi Press, 2006.

Dye, Robert W. *Shelby County*. Charleston, SC: Arcadia Publishing, 2005.

Gordon, Robert. *It Came from Memphis*. Boston: Faber and Faber, 1995.

Handy, W.C. *Father of the Blues: An Autobiography*. New York: Da Capo Press, 1941.

Harkins, John E. *Historic Shelby County: An Illustrated History*. San Antonio, TX: Historical Publishing Network, 2008.

————. *Metropolis of the American Nile: Memphis and Shelby County*. Memphis: West Tennessee Historical Society, 1982.

Honey, Michael K. *Going Down Jericho Road: The Memphis Strike, Martin Luther King's Last Campaign*. New York: W.W. Norton & Company, 2007.

Johnson, Eugene, and Robert Russell Jr. *Memphis: An Architectural Guide*. Knoxville: University of Tennessee Press, 1990.

Lanier, Robert. *Memphis in the Twenties: The Second Term of Mayor Rowlett Paine, 1924–1928*. Memphis, TN: Zenda Press, 1979.

Lauderdale, Vance. *Ask Vance*. Memphis, TN: Bluff City Books, 2003.

Lauterbach, Preston. *Beale Street Dynasty: Sex, Song, and the Struggle for the Soul of Memphis*. New York: W.W. Norton & Company, 2015.

Magness, Perre. *Good Abode: Nineteenth Century Architecture in Memphis and Shelby County, Tennessee*. Memphis, TN: Junior League of Memphis, 1983.

————. *Past Times: Stories of Early Memphis*. Memphis, TN: Parkway Press, 1996.

Matthews, Paul A., ed. *Early Families of the Memphis Area*. Nashville, TN: Panacea Press, 2008.

Raichelson, Richard. *Beale Street Talks*. Memphis, TN: Arcadia Records, 1999.

Robertson, David. *W.C. Handy: The Life and Times of the Man Who Made the Blues*. New York: Alfred A. Knopf, 2009.

Sanford, Otis. *From Boss Crump to King Willie: How Race Changed Memphis Politics*. Knoxville: University of Tennessee Press, 2017.

Sigafoos, Robert. *Cotton Row to Beale Street: A Business History of Memphis*. Memphis, TN: Memphis State University Press, 1964.

INDEX

W

Y

Z

ABOUT THE AUTHOR

Midtown resident Bill Patton is the founder of Memphis-based tour company Backbeat Tours (www.BackbeatTours.com). He is the author of *A Guide to Historic Downtown Memphis*, published by The History Press in 2010.